200 christmas

hamlyn | **all colour cookbook**

200 christmas recipes

An Hachette UK Company
www.hachette.co.uk

First published in Great Britain in 2009 by
Hamlyn, a division of Octopus Publishing Group Ltd,
2–4 Heron Quays, London E14 4JP
www.octopusbooks.co.uk

ISBN: 978-0-600-61938-3

A CIP catalogue record for this book is available
from the British Library.

Printed and bound in China

1 2 3 4 5 6 7 8 9 10

Both metric and imperial measurements have been given in all
recipes. Use one set of measurements only, not a mixture of both.

Standard level spoon measurements are used in all recipes
1 tablespoon = one 15 ml spoon
1 teaspoon = one 5 ml spoon

Ovens should be preheated to the specified temperature –
if using a fan assisted oven, follow the manufacturer's
instructions for adjusting the time and the temperature.

Fresh herbs should be used unless otherwise stated.

Medium eggs should be used unless otherwise stated. The
Department of Health advises that eggs should not be
consumed raw. This book contains some dishes made with raw
or lightly cooked eggs. It is prudent for vulnerable people such
as pregnant and nursing mothers, invalids, the elderly, babies
and young children to avoid uncooked or lightly cooked dishes
made with eggs. Once prepared, these dishes should be
kept refrigerated and used promptly.

This book also includes dishes made with nuts and nut
derivatives. It is advisable for those with known allergic
reactions to nuts and nut derivatives and those who may be
potentially vulnerable to these allergies, such as pregnant and
nursing mothers, invalids, the elderly, babies and children, to
avoid dishes made with nuts and nut oils. It is also prudent to
check the labels of pre-prepared ingredients for nut derivatives.

contents

introduction

introduction

Sharing fine food with friends and family is at the heart of Christmas and, although it can be hard work, preparing the festive offerings yourself is part of the fun. Cooking is a great way to channel all that pre-Christmas anticipation and get the whole family involved. Many families have their own traditions and it is festive rituals such as taking turns to stir the Christmas pudding mixture while making a wish that form the fondest memories.

festive fare

For many people, Roast Turkey (see page 18) is the centrepiece of the main festive meal, followed by Traditional Christmas Pudding (see page 80). Other favourites include Roast Goose with Spiced Apples (see page 36) and Roast Duckling with Clementines (see page 42). If you don't eat meat, there are special centrepiece recipes such as Honey & Citrus Roast Salmon (see page 38) or Feta and Roast Vegetable Tart (see page 44).

For other celebration meals over the festive period, you'll want something other than turkey and Christmas pudding. For example, you could greet your guests with Champagne Strawberry Cup (see page 100), then serve them a homemade Chicken Liver Pâté (see page 74) followed by Beef Wellington (see page 40) and Bombe Noël (see page 86) to finish. The 'Christmas Fare' chapter is packed with ideas for festive entertaining.

seasonal baking

Seasonal ingredients such as mincemeat, nuts, cranberries, dried fruits, marzipan and festive spices including cinnamon, nutmeg, ginger and cloves make Christmas baking special. Rich Mince Pies (see page 134) are a must and there are plenty of other festive goodies to make. Baking is a great way of involving children in the festive preparations. Even very little children can help use cookie cutters to cut out star shapes, trees and snowmen to make edible decorations for the Christmas tree (see pages 152 and 168), and afterwards they will enjoy hanging up the decorated biscuits with ribbon.

Cakes for Christmas come in all guises nowadays, from the fruit-packed Rich

Christmas Cake (see page 106) to novelty cakes to delight the children, such as the chocolate-crammed Santa's Sack (see page 108). If you would like a fruit Christmas cake, try to make it 1–3 months before Christmas. Store it in an airtight container and drizzle occasionally with a little brandy or sherry. You have the choice of leaving the cake un-iced or covering it with marzipan and a white icing. Other festive cakes include the marzipan-rich Pistachio Nut Stollen (see page 122), the deliciously chocolaty Bûche de Noël (see page 114) and the nut-packed Panforte Di Siena (see page 128).

making edible gifts

Homemade preserves, biscuits and sweets make great Christmas gifts and you'll find plenty of inspiration in the 'Edible Gifts' chapter. Creating attractive packaging is part of the fun. Look out for pretty gift boxes and line them with coordinating tissue paper to

prevent the biscuits or sweets from getting damaged. Alternatively, buy cellophane bags and secure them with invisible tape and festive ribbons and bows. If necessary, add a tag or label with storage instructions and a 'best before' date.

For homemade preserves you'll need to prepare the jars thoroughly. Sterilizing the jars is a crucial stage of making your own chutneys, pickles, jams and marmalades as the jars need to be spotlessly clean so the preserve will keep. Wash the jars in the dishwasher or alternatively wash them in hot soapy water, rinse and then dry them on the lowest setting in the oven for 15 minutes. Add the preserve to the still warm, dry jars, then press a disc of waxed paper, waxed side down, on to the surface of the preserve while it is still hot. Allow to cool, then add a cellophane cover and secure with a rubber band or add a sterilized screw-topped lid (this is essential in the case of chutney to stop the vinegar evaporating).

When the jars are filled and sealed, finish them with pretty seasonal jar covers and labels, available from good kitchenware shops. Label the jars with the name of the preserve, a 'best before' date and any recommended serving instructions.

madeira cake

Madeira cake is a good base for decorated novelty cakes. The recipe given on page 10 is required for the Christmas Stocking (see page 120), Smiling Snowman (see page 126) and Christmas Trees (see page 140). The

quantities given below make a 30 x 23 x 5 cm (12 x 9 x 2 inch) roasting-tin cake or 2 x 900 ml (1½ pint) pudding-basin cakes.

250 g (8 oz) **unsalted butter**, softened
250 g (8 oz) **caster sugar**
4 **eggs**
2 tablespoons **milk**
1 teaspoon **baking powder** (for roasting-tin cake only)
300 g (10 oz) **self-raising flour**
2 teaspoons **vanilla extract**

Cream the butter and sugar together in a large bowl until light and fluffy. Beat the eggs and milk together in a small bowl with a fork. If using, mix the baking powder with the flour.

Beat alternate spoonfuls of the egg mixture and the flour mixture into the creamed mixture until everything has been incorporated and the cake mixture is smooth. Beat in the vanilla extract. Spoon the cake mixture into a greased and lined 30 x 23 x

5 cm (12 x 9 x 2 inch) roasting tin or into 2 x 900 ml (1½ pint) pudding basins.

Bake in a preheated oven, 160°C (325°F), Gas Mark 3, for 30–35 minutes for the roasting tin and about 1 hour for the pudding basins, until well risen and golden brown and a skewer inserted into the centre of the cake comes out cleanly. Leave for 10 minutes, then loosen with a round-bladed knife, turn out on to a wire rack and leave to cool completely.

royal icing

Royal icing is the traditional icing used to cover celebration cakes. Depending on the consistency, it may be used for flat icing, peaked icing or for piping on as decoration. This recipe makes 500 g (1 lb) icing.

Glycerine, available from supermarkets, is often used in royal icing to help soften the icing but should be used sparingly. Royal icing contains raw egg, which should not be eaten by children, pregnant women, the elderly or those recovering from serious illness, unless it is pasteurized. Look out for pasteurized eggs in the supermarket chiller cabinet, but if these are unavailable, then make up powdered egg white instead (sold in tubs with other baking ingredients).

2 **egg whites**
¼ teaspoon **lemon juice**
500 g (1 lb) **icing sugar**, sieved
1 teaspoon **glycerine**

Place the egg whites and lemon juice in a clean bowl. Using a clean wooden spoon, stir to break up the egg whites. Add icing sugar to form the consistency of single cream. Continue mixing while adding small quantities of icing sugar until it is all used up, then stir in the glycerine until well blended. Cover with damp clingfilm, seal well to exclude all air, then allow to stand before using so air bubbles can rise to the surface and burst. Stir thoroughly, to disperse any air bubbles, then apply using a palette knife.

ready-to-roll (fondant) icing

Also known as fondant icing, ready-to-roll icing is readily available in white and a range of colours. You can also colour white ready-to-roll icing yourself by kneading in paste colouring, available from specialist cookshops. Roll out the icing, then cut shapes using a sharp knife or cookie cutters.

Ready-to-roll icing can also be used as an all-over smooth cake covering instead of royal icing. To cover a cake in ready-to-roll icing, first spread the top and sides of your cake with smooth apricot jam or butter icing. Knead the icing on a surface lightly dusted with icing sugar or cornflour to soften it slightly, then roll it out. When the icing is almost the same size as the top and sides of the cake, lift it over a rolling pin, then drape it over the cake. Working quickly, smooth the icing in place over the top of the cake and down to the board, with your fingertips dusted with icing sugar or cornflour. When the icing is in place, trim the excess from the base of the cake.

smooth apricot jam

Smooth apricot jam or economy jam doesn't contain fruit pieces so can be used straight from the jar for sticking marzipan and decorative icing directly on to cakes and biscuits. If the jam has a very set texture, warm it briefly in the microwave before using. Alternatively, warm fruity apricot jam in a saucepan with a little boiled water and then sieve it before use.

cutters

Plastic and metal cutters are useful for making shapes from ready-to-roll icing, biscuit and pastry dough and even cooled melted chocolate. Cutters come in a huge range of sizes and shapes. Ordinary round cutters have a myriad of uses. Gingerbread people are always popular shapes for biscuits and you can also buy special Christmas cutters, including Santa, star, bell, Christmas tree, angel, snowman, holly leaf, ivy leaf and

reindeer shapes. You can even get 3D cutters (see 3D Winter Wonderland, page 156).

Wash cutters after use with a small bottle brush and dry metal ones in the bottom of a cooling oven to avoid rusting. When using small cutters, dip them in a little icing sugar or cornflour before use to prevent sticking. To release cut-out shapes, press them out of the cutter using a fingertip or the rounded end of a small brush.

the turkey

A roast turkey and all the trimmings is often the focus of the main Christmas meal. The turkey is not difficult to cook but when there is so much else going on in the kitchen on Christmas morning, it's easy for the cook to become harassed.

Some forward planning will ensure smooth progress on the day. First work out the size of turkey you need to buy for the number of people you are catering for, allowing for approximately 500 g (1 lb) turkey weight per person. If it's to be a large turkey, make sure you check beforehand that your oven and roasting tin are big enough to take it.

There's a bewildering variety of turkeys available in the run-up to Christmas. Personal preference, availability and budget will influence where you buy it and whether you choose fresh or frozen, whole or jointed, ready-basted or pre-stuffed, organic or conventionally reared. Any of these options will taste delicious if cooked correctly. Whatever sort of turkey you choose, it should be at room temperature before it goes in the

oven and the cooking time should be based on its stuffed weight (see opposite).

fresh turkey

Fresh turkeys are available in supermarkets and butchers a week or so before Christmas, but it's best to order in advance to ensure you get the size you want.

If you're cooking for a small number or have only a small oven, consider buying a turkey joint instead of a whole turkey. A turkey crown is a whole turkey without the legs and wings, which gives you a joint of white breast meat on the bone. It's a popular choice as it is easy to carve and there's less wastage. Another option is a boned and rolled breast joint, which may come in netting to help it keep its shape. Remove the netting just before carving.

Remove the turkey from the refrigerator before you go to bed on Christmas Eve so that it comes up to room temperature and will heat up as soon as you put it in the oven. Once you have taken the turkey out, you can fill the refrigerator with all the drinks that need to be chilled for Christmas Day.

frozen turkey

If you're using a frozen turkey, allow plenty of time for the bird to defrost slowly and completely before you come to cook it. Depending on the size of your bird, transfer it from the freezer to the refrigerator 2–6 days in advance of Christmas Eve and leave it to defrost gradually, allowing 8–12 hours defrosting time per 1 kg (2 lb) turkey.

Once the turkey is defrosted and there are no ice crystals remaining, remove all the packaging and take out the giblets. Store these separately until required for giblet stock (see page 14). Place the defrosted bird in a deep dish near the bottom of the refrigerator to prevent uncooked turkey juices dripping on to anything else. Then, as with a fresh bird, take the defrosted turkey out of the refrigerator at the last possible moment on Christmas Eve to allow it to come to room temperature before cooking.

TURKEY COOKING GUIDE

To calculate the cooking time at 190°C (375°F), Gas Mark 5, allow 20 minutes per 1 kg (2 lb), plus 70 minutes for birds under 4 kg (8½ lb), or plus 90 minutes for birds weighing 4 kg (8½ lb) or more. These times apply whether you are cooking a whole stuffed bird or any turkey joint.

Turkey weight	Number of servings	Total cooking time
2 kg (4½ lb)	4–5	1 hour 50 minutes
2.5 kg (5½ lb)	5–6	2 hours
3 kg (6½ lb)	6–7	2 hours 10 minutes
3.5 kg (7½ lb)	7–8	2 hours 20 minutes
4 kg (8½ lb)	8–9	2 hours 50 minutes
4.5 kg (10 lb)	9–10	3 hours
5 kg (11 lb)	10–11	3 hours 10 minutes
5.5 kg (12 lb)	11–12	3 hours 20 minutes
6 kg (13 lb)	12–13	3 hours 30 minutes
6.5 kg (14 lb)	13–14	3 hours 40 minutes
7 kg (15½ lb)	14–15	3 hours 50 minutes
7.5 kg (16½ lb)	15–16	4 hours

cooking turkey to perfection

Make your chosen stuffing (see pages 22 and 24), then pack it loosely into the neck of the turkey – loosely because tightly packed stuffing would prevent heat penetrating the centre of the turkey. Similarly, don't stuff the body cavity of a whole bird as this may prevent it from cooking through completely. If you wish, place an onion, fresh herbs or slices of lemon or orange in the body cavity, to provide the meat with additional flavours.

This book describes how to cook a perfect Roast Turkey (see page 18) and Stuffed Turkey Breast Joint (see page 20). It is important to weigh the stuffed turkey to calculate the cooking time (see page 13) in a preheated oven, 190°C (375°F), Gas Mark 5.

For tender meat, rub the bird all over with softened butter before cooking or cover the breast and legs with rashers of bacon. Cover loosely with foil before cooking, then, during cooking, baste with the cooking juices from time to time. Forty minutes before the end of cooking, remove the foil (discard the bacon if using), baste the turkey and return to the oven uncovered to allow the skin to become crisp and brown.

is it cooked?

Check that a turkey (or other bird) is cooked by inserting a skewer into the thickest part of the thigh. The juices should run clear. If pink, cook for a further 15 minutes and test again. Transfer the bird to a large dish, cover with clean foil and leave to rest for 15–20 minutes. This resting time allows muscle fibres to relax

and become more tender, making the turkey easier to carve. Don't worry – its size means your roast turkey will not go cold quickly.

carving the bird

Using a sharp knife, cut the skin between legs and breast. Bend each leg outwards, cut through the joint and remove the whole leg – it should fall away easily. Remove the wings in the same way. Now make a horizontal cut at the base of the breast as far as the bone, then cut downwards to produce even slices of breast meat. Lastly, holding each drumstick in turn, slice the dark meat off the legs.

giblet stock

Giblet stock is the perfect base for gravy. Discard the liver (which can be bitter) and place the giblets of a turkey or other bird in a saucepan with 1 small quartered onion and

1.2 litres (2 pints) cold water. Bring to the boil, reduce the heat, cover and simmer for 1 hour. Strain the stock into a jug.

leftover turkey

Cooked turkey can be kept in the refrigerator in foil or clingfilm for up to 3 days. You can also freeze cooked turkey slices. Freezing in stock or gravy helps keep the meat moist. If you love turkey on Christmas Day but despair of what to do afterwards, turn to the 'Leftover Turkey Ideas' chapter for inspiration. From Rigatoni with Turkey & Pesto (page 218) to Turkey Curry (page 228) and Country Turkey Pie (see page 232), you should find some appealing recipes to tempt the family.

boning a whole turkey

A boned turkey makes a wonderful casing for stuffing, a joint of meat or another bird. A boned cavity and breast (see Steps 1–7) can be stuffed and re-formed so it looks like a conventional bird when cooked. Continue boning the rest of the bird (Steps 8–9) to make a classic ballotine or galantine. A proper boning knife will make the task easy.

1 Cut off the ends of the legs and wings at the first joints.

2 Lift back the neck skin and cut out the wishbone and any surrounding fat.

3 Place the bird breast side down on the board and cut along the backbone, working from the tail to the neck end.

4 Holding the knife blade angled towards the carcass, scrape away the flesh from the ribcage, working down one side of the bird to the wing.

5 Ease the knife between the ball and socket joint and sever from the ribcage, while keeping it attached to the skin.

6 Continue easing away the flesh from the bone, using small scraping cuts, until you reach the leg joint, then sever the ball and socket joint in the same way as you dealt with the wing. Continue in this way until you have reached the ridge of the breastbone. Then turn the bird around and repeat Steps 1–6 on the other side.

7 Pull gently to separate the breastbone from the skin. There is no flesh here, so take care not to tear the skin along the breastbone ridge or the bird will split open during cooking.

8 Lay the bird flat on the board, skin side down. Hold the outside of a wing bone and scrape away the flesh. Work top to bottom, severing tendons as you go. Pull out the wing bone. Repeat on the other wing. Push the skin and flesh of the wings back inside the carcass to make a neater parcel for stuffing.

9 Hold the inside of the leg bone and scrape away the flesh with a pencil-sharpening action. Sever tendons as you go, then release the bone when you get to the bottom of the leg. Repeat with the other leg.

christmas
fare

roast turkey

Serves **10**, with leftovers
Preparation time **30 minutes**
Cooking time **3 hours**
 15 minutes–3 hours
 40 minutes, according
 to weight

1 quantity **Pecan Stuffing**
 (see page 22) or **Cranberry
 & Orange Stuffing** (see
 page 24)
5–6 kg (11–13 lb) **oven-
 ready turkey**, giblets
 removed and cavity wiped
 clean
1 small **onion**, halved
40 g (1½ oz) **butter**, softened
2 tablespoons **vegetable oil**
3 **thyme sprigs**, chopped
salt and **pepper**

Pack your chosen stuffing loosely into the neck of the
bird and secure the neck flap with 2 crossed skewers.
Place the onion in the body cavity and season the
cavity with salt and pepper. Tie the turkey legs together
with string at the top of the drumsticks.

Weigh the stuffed turkey to calculate the cooking time
(see page 13), then place the bird in a large roasting
tin. Rub all over with softened butter and season the
outside of the turkey. Add the vegetable oil to the tin.

Cover the prepared turkey loosely with foil and roast
in a preheated oven, 190°C (375°F), Gas Mark 5, for
the required cooking time, basting from time to time.
Remove the foil for the last 40 minutes of cooking to
brown the bird and scatter over the chopped thyme.
Check the turkey is cooked (see page 14).

Transfer the turkey to a large dish, cover with clean foil
and leave to rest for 15–20 minutes before carving.
Meanwhile, pour off the fat from the roasting tin and
use the juices to make gravy (see page 26).

Arrange the turkey on a warmed serving platter and
serve with all the traditional accompaniments, such as
Bacon & Chipolata Rolls (see page 26), Bread Sauce
(see page 28), Brandied Cranberry Sauce (see page
30) and an assortment of vegetables.

stuffed turkey breast joint

Serves **7–8**

Preparation time **30 minutes**

Cooking time **3 hours**, or according to weight

3.5 kg (7½ lb) **skin-on boned breast joint**

125 g (4 oz) **butter**, softened

1 **bay leaf**

2 tablespoons **vegetable oil**

salt and **pepper**

Stuffing

1 tablespoon **vegetable oil**

½ large **onion**, finely chopped

1 **celery stick**, finely chopped

175 g (6 oz) **mixed dried fruit**, finely chopped

175 g (6 oz) **fresh breadcrumbs**

125 g (4 oz) **mixed shelled nuts**, finely chopped

½ medium **cooking apple**, peeled, cored and grated

1 tablespoon chopped **parsley**

½ tablespoon chopped **thyme**

1 **egg**, beaten

Heat the oil for the stuffing in a pan, add the onion and celery and fry over a gentle heat, stirring frequently, for about 10 minutes until softened. Turn into a bowl, add the remaining stuffing ingredients with salt and pepper to taste and mix well together. Set aside.

Ease your fingers between the turkey skin and the breast meat. Push in the softened butter to cover the breast completely. Place the turkey skin side down, season with salt and pepper, then spread with the stuffing. Bring the turkey up and around the stuffing to enclose it, making as neat and compact a shape as possible, and secure with string. Tuck a bay leaf under the string.

Weigh the stuffed turkey to calculate the cooking time (see page 13), add the vegetable oil to the roasting tin, then place the turkey breast side up in the roasting tin. Cover loosely with foil and roast in a preheated oven, 190°C (375°F), Gas Mark 5, for the calculated cooking time or until the juices run clear when the thickest part is pierced with a skewer (see page 14). Remove the foil for the last 40 minutes of cooking to brown the bird.

Lift the turkey out of the tin, cover tightly with foil and rest in a warm place for 15–20 minutes before serving. Meanwhile, pour off the fat from the roasting tin and use the juices to make gravy (see page 26). Place the turkey on a warmed serving platter to serve.

pecan stuffing

Makes **enough for a 6 kg
 (13 lb) turkey**
Preparation time **5 minutes**
Cooking time **15 minutes**,
 plus turkey cooking time

heart and **liver** from a 6 kg
 (13 lb) **turkey**
50 g (2 oz) **fresh
 breadcrumbs**
50 g (2 oz) **shelled pecan
 nuts**, finely chopped
1 **egg**, hard-boiled and
 chopped
pinch of grated **nutmeg**
pinch of **ground mace**
1 tablespoon chopped **thyme**
1 tablespoon chopped
 parsley
pinch of **celery salt**
40 g (1½ oz) **butter**
50 g (2 oz) **mushrooms**,
 finely chopped
1 small **onion**, chopped
2 tablespoons **dry sherry**
salt and **pepper**

Put the heart and liver in a saucepan and cover with water. Bring to the boil and simmer for 10 minutes. Chop the meat finely and set aside to cool.

Place the chopped meat in a bowl and stir in the breadcrumbs, nuts, egg, spices, herbs and celery salt.

Melt the butter in a saucepan, add the mushrooms and onion and cook over a moderate heat, stirring frequently, for about 5 minutes until softened. Stir into the meat mixture, add the sherry and season to taste.

Pack the stuffing loosely into the neck of the turkey (see page 18) or shape into small balls and place in the tin around the turkey for the last 30 minutes of the turkey's cooking time.

For sweet potato & sausagemeat stuffing, melt 25 g (1 oz) butter in a frying pan and fry 1 chopped onion and 2 chopped celery sticks until softened. Tip into a bowl and allow to cool, then stir in 300 g (10 oz) peeled and grated sweet potato, 500 g (1 lb) pork sausagemeat, the grated rind of 1 lemon and 15 g (½ oz) chopped herbs (such as parsley, oregano, sage, thyme). Mix well and finish cooking as above.

cranberry & orange stuffing

Makes **enough for a 6 kg (13 lb) turkey**
Preparation time **10 minutes**
Cooking time **13–16 minutes**, plus turkey cooking time

75 g (3 oz) **sugar**
150 ml (¼ pint) **water**
grated rind and juice of
  1 **orange**
250 g (8 oz) fresh or frozen
  cranberries, defrosted if
  frozen
375 g (12 oz) mixed **long-grain** and **wild rice**
75 g (3 oz) **butter**
1 large **onion**, finely chopped
2 tablespoons chopped
  parsley
1 tablespoon chopped **thyme**
pinch of **ground cloves**
pinch of grated **nutmeg**
salt and **pepper**

Put the sugar and water into a saucepan and stir over a low heat until the sugar is dissolved. Bring to the boil and boil for 2–3 minutes. Add the orange rind and juice and the cranberries and stir with a wooden spoon, taking care not to crush the fruit. Simmer for 5 minutes until the sauce is translucent. Set aside.

Meanwhile cook the rice in a large pan of boiling salted water for 10–12 minutes until just tender. Drain, rinse under cold water and drain again.

Melt the butter in a saucepan and fry the onion over a moderate heat for 3–4 minutes, stirring once or twice. Remove from the heat.

Stir the rice, herbs, spices and cranberry and orange mixture into the onions. Season with salt and pepper and set aside to cool before packing loosely into the neck of the turkey (see page 18). Alternatively, cook in the oven for the last 30 minutes of the turkey's cooking time, either separately in an ovenproof dish or shaped into small balls and placed in the tin around the turkey.

For blueberry & orange stuffing, omit the cranberries and instead add 250 g (8 oz) blueberries to the dissolved sugar with the orange rind and juice, then continue with the recipe as above. Defrost first if using frozen blueberries.

bacon & chipolata rolls

Makes **16**
Preparation time **5 minutes**
Cooking time **16–20 minutes**

16 rindless **streaky bacon
rashers**
16 **pork chipolata sausages**

Stretch out the rashers of streaky bacon using the back of a knife, then wind a rasher along the length of each sausage.

Cook under a medium grill for about 8–10 minutes on each side. Serve at least 2 per person alongside the Christmas roast.

For wine gravy, to serve with the turkey and trimmings, first make a stock from the giblets (see page 14) and set aside. While the cooked turkey is resting, spoon out all but 2 tablespoons of the fat from the roasting tin. Stir in 2 tablespoons plain flour and cook gently on the hob, stirring, for 1–2 minutes until golden. Add 50 ml (¼ pint) full-bodied red wine, 450 ml (¾ pint) hot giblet stock, a few drops of gravy browning, 2 tablespoons redcurrant jelly and salt and pepper. Simmer, stirring, for 5 minutes, then serve.

For thin gravy, follow the recipe above but pour off *all* the fat from the roasting tin, leaving behind the sediment and pan juices. Set over a high heat and pour in 900 ml (1½ pints) hot giblet stock. Boil until reduced by about one-third. Reduce the heat to moderate, whisk in the finely grated rind and juice of 2 oranges, 4 tablespoons port or sherry, 2 tablespoons cranberry sauce or jelly and salt and pepper. Simmer, stirring, for a few minutes, then serve.

bread sauce

Serves **8**
Preparation time **10 minutes**,
  plus infusing
Cooking time **15–20 minutes**

1 small **onion**
3 whole **cloves**, plus extra to
  garnish (optional)
1 **bay leaf**, plus 1 to garnish
  (optional)
a few **parsley sprigs**
450 ml (¾ pint) **milk**
75 g (3 oz) **fresh white
  breadcrumbs**
40 g (1½ oz) **butter**
150 ml (¼ pint) **single cream**
grated **nutmeg**
salt and **pepper**

Stud the onion with the cloves and place it in a
saucepan with the bay leaf, parsley and milk. Cover
and bring slowly to the boil to allow the milk to better
absorb the flavours. Remove the pan from the heat and
leave to infuse for 30 minutes.

Strain into a clean pan, discarding the onion and herbs.
Stir in the breadcrumbs and butter and cook over a
very low heat, stirring occasionally, for 15 minutes. Stir
in the cream and add nutmeg and salt and pepper to
taste. Garnish with a bay leaf and 2 or 3 cloves, if liked,
and a final grating of nutmeg.

For reduced-fat bread sauce, follow the recipe
above but omit the single cream and instead stir in
150 ml (¼ pint) half-fat crème fraîche before adding
the nutmeg and seasoning.

brandied cranberry sauce

Serves **6**
Preparation time **5 minutes**
Cooking time **5–10 minutes**

125 g (4 oz) fresh or frozen
  cranberries, defrosted if
  frozen
150 ml (¼ pint) **water**
2 tablespoons **light brown
  sugar**
pared rind of 1 **orange**
2 tablespoons **brandy**

Mix the cranberries, water, light brown sugar, orange rind and brandy together in a saucepan.

Cover the pan and cook over a low heat, stirring, for 5–10 minutes, until the cranberries burst.

For cranberry & orchard fruit sauce, finely chop 1–2 dessert apples or pears and place in a saucepan with the cranberries, water, light brown sugar, grated orange rind and brandy. Cook as above until the cranberries burst.

roast beef sirloin

Serves **6–8**

Preparation time **15 minutes**, plus marinating

Cooking time **1 hour–1 hour 40 minutes**

1.5–2 kg (3–4½ lb) **boneless beef sirloin**

3 tablespoons **olive oil**

1 tablespoon **lemon juice**

1 large **onion**, thinly sliced

2 large **thyme sprigs** or **rosemary sprigs**

salt and **pepper**

Dry the meat well. Rub it all over with the oil and drizzle over the lemon juice. Place half the onion slices and 1 thyme sprig in a dish, put the beef on top and cover with the remaining onions and thyme sprig. Season with salt and pepper. Cover and leave the beef in a cool place to marinate for at least 3 hours.

Discard the onions. Place the beef on a rack over a roasting tin to catch the meat juices. Put into the top of a preheated oven, 220°C (425°F), Gas Mark 7. For rare beef, allow 15 minutes per 500 g (1 lb) plus 15 minutes. For medium-done beef, allow 20 minutes per 500 g (1 lb) plus 20 minutes. After 1 hour of cooking, reduce the temperature to 190°C (375°F), Gas Mark 5. Baste occasionally with the pan juices.

Remove the beef from the roasting tin and allow it to rest on the rack, covered with a tent of foil. Carve the beef into slices and serve with Red Wine Sauce (see below) and roast potatoes and vegetables, if liked.

For red wine sauce, to serve with the sirloin, melt 25 g (1 oz) butter in a pan, add 6 finely chopped shallots and cook until softened but not browned. Add 300 ml (½ pint) red wine and 300 ml (½ pint) beef or vegetable stock. Bring to the boil, reduce the heat and simmer for 20–30 minutes until reduced by half. Add 2 tablespoons chopped parsley and season with salt and pepper. Remove from the heat and gradually whisk in 50 g (2 oz) butter. Add a little sugar if the sauce seems acidic.

moroccan stuffed lamb

Serves **8–10**
Preparation time
 15–20 minutes
Cooking time **50 minutes**

2 kg (4½ lb) **boned leg of lamb**
1 **onion**, cut in thick wedges
3 tablespoons **olive oil**
8 tablespoons **lemon juice**
pepper

Moroccan stuffing
150 ml (¼ pint) boiling **water**
50 g (2 oz) **couscous**
2 teaspoons **coriander seeds**
2 teaspoons **cumin seeds**
1 teaspoon **ground cinnamon**
3 tablespoons **olive oil**
50 g (2 oz) **pine nuts**
50 g (2 oz) **flaked almonds**
1 large **onion**, finely chopped
2 **garlic cloves**, crushed
1 teaspoon **dried mint**
4 tablespoons chopped **coriander leaves**
50 g (2 oz) **raisins**
salt and **pepper**

Pour the boiling water over the couscous, stir, then leave until absorbed. Heat the coriander and cumin seeds in a small pan until fragrant. Grind to a powder, then mix with the cinnamon. Heat 1 tablespoon of the oil in a frying pan, add the pine nuts and almonds and fry until browned. Transfer to kitchen paper to drain. Add the remaining oil to the pan. When hot, add the onion and fry until soft. Stir in the garlic and spice mixture and fry for 2 minutes, then add the nuts, mint, coriander, raisins, couscous and salt and pepper.

Open out the lamb, skin side down, on a work surface. Season inside with pepper, then spread over the stuffing. If possible, tuck the flaps of the piece of lamb over the stuffing. Roll up the lamb into a neat sausage shape, then tie it securely with string.

Put the onion wedges into a roasting tin in which the lamb will just fit. Place the lamb on top of the onion wedges and pour over the oil and lemon juice. Cook in a preheated oven, 240°C (475°F), Gas Mark 9, for 15 minutes, then reduce the temperature to 220°C (425°F), Gas Mark 7, and cook for a further 25 minutes, so that the lamb is pink in the centre. Remove the lamb from the oven, cover and leave to stand in a warm place for about 15 minutes before carving.

For lamb stuffed with figs & orange, omit the stuffing above and instead combine 300 g (10 oz) chopped dried figs, 125 g (4 oz) fresh breadcrumbs, 1 finely chopped onion, 2 teaspoons grated orange rind, 100 ml (3½ fl oz) orange juice, ½ teaspoon ground cinnamon and salt and pepper. Stuff and cook the lamb as above. Serve garnished with sliced figs.

roast goose with spiced apples

Serves **8**

Preparation time **35 minutes**

Cooking time **3¾ hours**

5–6 kg (11–13 lb) **oven-ready goose**, plus giblets

1 **onion**, halved

1 **carrot**

1 **celery stick**

1.2 litres (2 pints) **water**

50 g (2 oz) **butter**

1 large **onion**, chopped

375 g (12 oz) **dried figs**, chopped

175 g (6 oz) **fresh breadcrumbs**

2 tablespoons chopped **parsley**

2 tablespoons chopped **thyme**

1 **egg**

8 small **apples**, cored

16 whole **cloves**

25 g (1 oz) **light muscovado sugar**

½ teaspoon **ground mixed spice**

salt and **pepper**

Put the giblets in a saucepan, discarding the liver. Add the halved onion, carrot, celery and measured water. Bring to the boil, reduce the heat and simmer gently for 1 hour. Strain the giblet stock and reserve.

Melt half the butter and fry the onion for 3 minutes. Remove from the heat and add 250 g (8 oz) of the figs and the breadcrumbs, parsley, thyme and egg. Season lightly and mix well. Pack half the stuffing into the neck end. Shape the remaining stuffing into 2.5 cm (1 inch) balls.

Tuck the skin flap under the bird and truss it, with the wings folded under the body and the legs tied together with string. Place on a rack over a roasting tin. Roast the goose in a preheated oven, 180°C (350°F), Gas Mark 4, for 2¾ hours.

Cut a thin slice off the top of each apple and stud with 2 whole cloves. Combine the remaining figs, sugar and mixed spice and pack into and on top of the apples. Melt the remaining butter and pour it over the apples.

Place the apples and stuffing in the oven 30 minutes before the end of the goose roasting time, basting the apples frequently with the butter. Test the goose to see if it is cooked (see page 14). Transfer to a warmed serving dish and add the spiced apples and stuffing balls. Keep warm.

Pour off all the fat from the roasting tin. Add 600 ml (1 pint) reserved giblet stock, making up with water if necessary. Bring to the boil and season lightly with salt and pepper. Strain and serve with the goose.

honey & citrus roast salmon

Serves **6**
Preparation time **10 minutes**,
  plus marinating
Cooking time **20 minutes**

1.25 kg (2½ lb) **side of
  salmon**
thinly pared rind and juice of
  1 orange
2 tablespoons **clear honey**
thinly pared rind of **1 lemon**
25 g (1 oz) **butter**
salt and **pepper**

To garnish
1 lemon, cut into wedges
a few **watercress sprigs**

Lay the salmon in a lightly greased baking tray. Stir the orange juice into the honey and brush the mixture over the salmon. Cut the orange and lemon rind into thin strips and scatter them over the salmon. Leave to marinate in the refrigerator for 30 minutes.

Season the salmon with salt and pepper, then bake in a preheated oven, 200°C (400°F), Gas Mark 6, for 20 minutes, until cooked through.

Transfer the salmon on to a serving platter and garnish with lemon wedges and watercress sprigs. Serve with new potatoes, if liked.

For salmon & cream cheese pâté, blend any left-over roast salmon with cream cheese in a food processor (or finely flake the salmon and stir in the cream cheese). You'll need 1 part cheese to 2 parts cooked salmon. Once well combined, stir in 2 tablespoons snipped chives and season with salt and pepper. Serve as a canapé on small triangles of toasted brown bread, if liked.

beef wellington

Serves **6**
Preparation time **30 minutes**
Cooking time about **1 hour**

1.5 kg (3 lb) **beef fillet**
   (preferably cut from the
   middle of the fillet)
50 g (2 oz) **butter**
2 small **onions**, finely chopped
300 g (10 oz) **chestnut
   mushrooms**, chopped
2 tablespoons **brandy**
500 g (1 lb) **ready-made puff
   pastry**, defrosted if frozen
a little **flour**, for dusting
200 g (7 oz) **smooth chicken
   pâté**
beaten **egg**, to glaze
salt and **pepper**

Trim off the excess fat and season the beef. Melt the butter in a frying pan and sear the beef on all sides. Transfer it to a roasting tin, reserving the fat in the pan, and roast in a preheated oven, 200°C (400°F), Gas Mark 6, for 20 minutes. Leave to cool.

Fry the onions in the pan for 5 minutes while the beef is cooking. Add the mushrooms and a little seasoning and fry until the moisture has evaporated. Add the brandy and fry for a further 1 minute. Leave to cool.

Thinly roll out the pastry to a large rectangle on a lightly floured surface. Spread the top of the meat with the chicken pâté, then press a thick layer of the mushroom mixture over the top. Invert the beef on to the pastry and spread with the remaining mushrooms.

Brush the pastry with beaten egg and bring it up over the fillet to enclose the meat completely, trimming off any bulky areas at the corners. Place, join side down, on a lightly greased baking sheet and brush with more egg. Bake for 35 minutes, until deep golden. Leave to stand for 20 minutes before carving.

For individual beef Wellingtons, lightly sear 4 x 150–175 g (5–6 oz) fillet steaks in a hot pan for 30 seconds on each side. Allow to cool. Divide 375 g (12 oz) puff pastry into 4 and roll out each piece to a rectangle. Place a steak on each pastry rectangle. Season the steaks, then spread with 200 g (7 oz) mushroom pâté. Enclose the meat in the pastry and continue as above, cooking for 25–30 minutes.

roast duckling with clementines

Serves **4**

Preparation time
20–25 minutes

Cooking time **2 hours**

2.5 kg (5½ lb) **oven-ready duckling**
½ teaspoon **ground allspice**
25 g (1 oz) **butter**
pared rind and juice of
  1 orange
2 **cinnamon sticks**, halved
4 **clementines**, peeled but left whole
175 g (6 oz) fresh or frozen **cranberries**, defrosted if frozen
5 tablespoons **light muscovado sugar**
2 teaspoons **white wine vinegar**
2 tablespoons **Cointreau**
salt and **pepper**
bay leaves, to garnish (optional)

Pierce the duckling all over, except the breast area, to release the fat during cooking. Rub the skin with allspice and sprinkle with salt and pepper. Place on a rack over a roasting tin and cook in a preheated oven, 220°C (425°F), Gas Mark 7, for 15 minutes. Reduce the temperature to 190°C (375°F), Gas Mark 5, and cook for a further 1 hour.

Melt the butter in a small saucepan. Add the orange rind, cinnamon sticks and whole clementines and cook for 1 minute. Place the clementines and orange rind around the duckling and pour over the remaining butter. Return to the oven for a further 45 minutes.

Pour the orange juice and cranberries into the butter saucepan. Simmer gently for about 10 minutes, until the cranberries pop.

Put the duckling, cinnamon sticks, clementines and orange rind in a serving dish. Garnish the dish with bay leaves (if liked) and keep warm. Drain the fat from the roasting tin, then add the cranberries and juice, sugar, vinegar and Cointreau. Bring to the boil, stirring. Season to taste and serve with the duckling.

For roast duckling with kumquats, prepare the bird as above but rub with salt instead of allspice. Tuck 3 tarragon sprigs and 4 kumquats from a total weight of 250 g (8 oz) inside the duckling and cook as above. A few minutes before it is cooked, halve the remaining kumquats and place in a pan with 1 tablespoon each orange juice and clear honey and 3 tablespoons sherry. Bring to the boil and cook gently for 2 minutes, stirring. Spoon on top of the duckling and serve.

feta & roast vegetable tart

Serves **6**
Preparation time **25 minutes**,
  plus chilling
Cooking time about **1 hour**

125 g (4 oz) **self-raising flour**
50 g (2 oz) **oatmeal**
75 g (3 oz) chilled **butter**,
  diced
about 2 tablespoons cold
  water
1 **aubergine**, sliced
1 **red pepper**, cored,
  deseeded and cut into thick
  strips
1 **onion**, cut into wedges
2 **courgettes**, cut into sticks
3 **tomatoes**, halved
2 **garlic cloves**, chopped
3 tablespoons **olive oil**
2 teaspoons chopped
  rosemary
125 g (4 oz) **feta cheese**,
  crumbled
2 tablespoons freshly grated
  Parmesan cheese
salt and **pepper**

Mix the flour and oatmeal in a bowl, then add the butter and rub in until the mixture resembles fine breadcrumbs. Add the water and mix to a firm dough. Turn out on to a lightly floured surface and knead briefly.

Roll out the pastry and line a 23 cm (9 inch) fluted flan tin, pressing evenly into the sides. Prick the base with a fork, chill for 15 minutes, then line with nonstick baking paper and add macaroni or baking beans. Bake blind in a preheated oven, 190°C (375°F), Gas Mark 5, for 10–15 minutes. Remove the paper and macaroni or beans and return to the oven for 5 minutes.

Mix the vegetables in a roasting tin. Add the garlic, oil and rosemary, coating the vegetables evenly. Season to taste. Roast at 200°C (400°F), Gas Mark 6, for 35 minutes or until the vegetables are tender.

Fill the pastry case with the cooked vegetables, scatter the feta cheese over the top and sprinkle with the Parmesan. Return the tart to the oven for 10 minutes.

For roast pepper & haloumi tart, bake the pastry case as above, meanwhile roasting 2 large red, 2 large orange and 2 large yellow peppers, all cut into thick strips, with the garlic, oil, rosemary and seasoning. Spread 6 tablespoons pesto over the base of the pastry case, then top with the peppers. Sprinkle with 50 g (2 oz) pitted black olives. Omit the feta cheese and arrange 125 g (4 oz) thinly sliced haloumi cheese over the top. Bake for a further 10 minutes as above.

pasta-packed baked red peppers

Serves **4**
Preparation time **20 minutes**
Cooking time **35–45 minutes**

4 **red peppers**, halved, cored
    and deseeded
125 g (4 oz) **mini macaroni**,
    cooked
2 **plum tomatoes**, chopped
125 g (4 oz) **Cheddar
    cheese**, grated
2 **spring onions**, sliced
2 tablespoons chopped
    parsley
3 tablespoons **olive oil**
salt and **pepper**

Place the halved peppers in an ovenproof dish, hollows uppermost. Mix the macaroni, tomatoes, cheese, spring onions and parsley in a bowl. Spoon into the peppers, drizzle with the olive oil and season to taste.

Bake in a preheated oven, 180°C (350°F), Gas Mark 4, for 35–45 minutes or until the macaroni filling is golden and bubbling.

For baked stuffed mushrooms, remove and finely chop the stalks from 4 large field mushrooms. Grill the mushrooms for 5 minutes until just softened. Finely chop 1 small onion and mix with the chopped mushroom stalks, 50 g (2 oz) cooked macaroni, 25 g (1 oz) chopped walnuts, 1 tablespoon chopped parsley, 25 g (1 oz) cubed Cheddar cheese and 1 tablespoon tomato purée. Season, then bind with a little beaten egg. Pile on top of the mushrooms, drizzle with a little olive oil, then cook under a preheated medium grill for 15–20 minutes until the top of the stuffing is crisp and has started to char at the edges.

melanzane parmigiana

Serves **6**

Preparation time **10 minutes**, plus draining

Cooking time **1 hour 25 minutes**

6 **aubergines**, cut lengthways into thick slices

2 tablespoons **extra virgin olive oil**

250 g (8 oz) **Cheddar cheese**, grated

50 g (2 oz) freshly grated **Parmesan cheese**

salt

Tomato sauce

1 kg (2 lb) ripe **tomatoes**, roughly chopped

2 tablespoons **extra virgin olive oil**

2 **garlic cloves**, chopped

2 tablespoons chopped **basil**

1 teaspoon grated **lemon rind**

pinch of **sugar**

salt and **pepper**

Sprinkle the aubergines with salt and leave to drain in a colander for 30 minutes. Wash well, drain and pat dry on kitchen paper.

Bring all the ingredients for the tomato sauce to the boil. Cover and simmer for 30 minutes. Remove the lid and cook for a further 20 minutes until the sauce is thick. Adjust the seasoning.

Meanwhile brush the slices of aubergine with the oil and place on 2 large baking sheets. Roast at the top of a preheated oven, 200°C (400°F), Gas Mark 6, for 10 minutes on each side until golden and tender.

Spoon a little tomato sauce into 6 lightly greased individual ovenproof dishes (or 1 lasagne dish) and top with a layer of aubergines and some Cheddar. Continue the layers, finishing with the Cheddar. Sprinkle the Parmesan over the top and bake at 200°C (400°F), Gas Mark 6, for 30 minutes until bubbling and golden.

For aubergine layer pasta, slice, salt, rinse and roast 3 sliced aubergines as above. Fry 1 chopped onion in 1 tablespoon olive oil for 5 minutes, then add 1½ tablespoons each chopped oregano and basil, 175 g (6 oz) sliced mushrooms and 825 g (1 lb 11 oz) passata. Simmer for 10 minutes, then season. In an ovenproof dish, arrange 4–5 lasagne sheets, then add one-third of the tomato sauce, one-third of the aubergines, one-third of 550 g (18 oz) sliced mozzarella and one-third of 175 g (6 oz) grated Gruyère. Repeat the layering twice. Cover with foil and bake at 190°C (375°F), Gas Mark 5, for 45 minutes. Remove the foil after 20 minutes to brown the top.

sesame roast potatoes

Serves **4**
Preparation time **10 minutes**
Cooking time **1–1¼ hours**

4 **baking potatoes**,
  175–250 g (6–8 oz)
  each, peeled and halved
  lengthways
4 tablespoons **olive oil**
2 tablespoons **sesame seeds**
salt

Place the potatoes cut side down. Using a sharp knife, make cuts at 5 mm (¼ inch) intervals along the length of each potato almost through to the base, so that they just hold together.

Heat the oil in a roasting tin in a preheated oven, 200°C (400°F), Gas Mark 6, until hot. Add the potatoes to the tin and spoon over the oil evenly. Sprinkle with a little salt, baste well and roast the potatoes for 30 minutes.

Remove the potatoes from the oven, sprinkle with the sesame seeds, then return to the oven for a further 30 minutes until golden brown and crisp.

For garlic & thyme roast potatoes, remove the potatoes from the oven after 30 minutes and, instead of sprinkling with sesame seeds, add 8 unpeeled garlic cloves and 10–12 thyme sprigs to the roasting tin. Cook for a further 30 minutes, as above.

potatoes dauphinoise

Serves **4–6**
Preparation time **10 minutes**
Cooking time **1–1¼ hours**

750 g–1 kg (1½–2 lb) evenly
  shaped **potatoes**, peeled
  and thinly sliced
1 teaspoon grated **nutmeg**
1 **garlic clove**, crushed
300 ml (½ pint) **double cream**
75 g (3 oz) **Gruyère** or
  Cheddar cheese, grated
salt and **pepper**

Arrange the potatoes in layers in a well-greased ovenproof dish, sprinkling each layer with nutmeg, salt and pepper.

Stir the crushed garlic clove into the cream and pour the cream over the potatoes. Sprinkle the cheese over the surface so that the potatoes are completely covered. Cover with foil and bake in a preheated oven, 180°C (350°F), Gas Mark 4, for 45 minutes.

Remove the foil and cook for 15–30 minutes more, or until the potatoes are cooked through and the cheese topping is crusty and golden brown.

For potato & leek bake, place 500 g (1 lb) sliced leeks in the bottom of the dish before adding the layers of potatoes. Add the nutmeg, seasoning, cream and garlic as above, then sprinkle 50 g (2 oz) grated Cheddar cheese mixed with 25 g (1 oz) fresh breadcrumbs over the top.

roast parsnips with thyme butter

Serves **4**
Preparation time **10 minutes**
Cooking time **40–45 minutes**

625 g (1¼ lb) **baby parsnips**, scrubbed
1 tablespoon **extra virgin olive oil**
1 **garlic clove**, crushed
2 **thyme sprigs**, chopped
1 teaspoon grated **lemon rind**
pinch of **cayenne pepper**
pinch of **sea salt**

Toss the parsnips with the oil, garlic, thyme sprigs, lemon rind, cayenne pepper and salt, and place in a roasting tin.

Bake in a preheated oven, 200°C (400°F), Gas Mark 6, for 40–45 minutes, stirring occasionally until golden and tender. Serve at once.

For roast butternut squash, cut a 1 kg (2 lb) squash in half lengthways, remove the seeds and fibrous centres and cut into wedges. Toss with 2 tablespoons virgin olive oil, the leaves from 2 large thyme sprigs and salt and pepper, and place in a roasting tin. Bake at the top of a preheated oven, 220°C (425°F), Gas Mark 7, for 20–25 minutes, basting halfway through the cooking time, until the squash is soft and slightly browned. Serve drizzled with a little pumpkin seed oil.

brussels sprouts with chestnuts

Serves **10**
Preparation time **10 minutes**
Cooking time **6–10 minutes**

1.5 kg (3 lb) **Brussels
  sprouts**
50 g (2 oz) **butter**
400 g (13 oz) vacuum-packed
  cooked, peeled **chestnuts**,
  halved
salt and **pepper**

Remove the tough outer leaves and place the sprouts in a pan of boiling salted water. Cover and cook gently for 6–10 minutes, depending on their size, until just tender. (Take care not to overcook them, as overcooked sprouts have an unpleasant taste and smell.)

Meanwhile melt the butter in a saucepan and add the chestnuts. Heat gently until warmed through.

Drain the sprouts and stir into the warmed chestnuts. Season with a little salt and pepper and serve.

For pan-fried Brussels sprouts, halve 1.5 kg (3 lb) sprouts if large, cook in boiling water for 3 minutes, then drain. Melt 50 g (2 oz) butter or bacon fat in a frying pan until sizzling, then add the sprouts and 2 crushed garlic cloves. Fry gently for 3 minutes. Season with grated nutmeg and salt and pepper and sprinkle with a handful of lightly toasted flaked almonds before serving.

glazed baby carrots

Serves **6**
Preparation time **5 minutes**
Cooking time **15–20 minutes**

50 g (2 oz) **butter**
1 kg (2 lb) whole **baby
   carrots**, or young ones
   quartered lengthways
generous pinch of **sugar**
juice of **1 orange**
salt and **pepper**
parsley, roughly chopped,
   to garnish

Melt the butter in a saucepan, add the carrots and
sugar and season with salt and pepper.

Pour in just enough water to cover the carrots and
cook gently, uncovered, for 10–12 minutes or until
the carrots are tender and the liquid has evaporated.
As the water evaporates, add the orange juice. Serve
garnished with the chopped parsley.

For carrots with ginger & orange butter, steam
or boil 1 kg (2 lb) carrots for 10–12 minutes until
tender. Meanwhile, mix 50 g (2 oz) softened butter,
1 teaspoon grated fresh root ginger, ½ teaspoon
grated orange rind, ½ tablespoon orange juice,
½ teaspoon clear honey, 1 tablespoon chopped
chervil and salt and pepper until smooth and evenly
combined. Toss the cooked carrots in the spiced
butter and serve at once.

roast courgettes with shallots

Serves **4–6**
Preparation time **5 minutes**
Cooking time **40 minutes**

1 kg (2 lb) **courgettes**
6 **shallots**, quartered, with
    root left intact
4 tablespoons **olive oil**
1 tablespoon **pumpkin seed
    oil** (optional)
salt and **pepper**

Cut the courgettes in half across the middle, then cut each piece in half again and then into quarters lengthways to make batons.

Place the courgette batons in a roasting tin and add the shallots. Mix the olive oil and the pumpkin seed oil, if using, and use to coat the courgette batons and shallots. (If you don't want to use pumpkin seed oil, use 5 tablespoons olive oil in total instead.) Season with salt and pepper and cook at the top of a preheated oven, 190°C (375°F), Gas Mark 5, for 40 minutes.

Baste the courgettes and shallots 2–3 times during cooking. Once cooked, the courgettes and shallots should be soft and speckled with brown.

For courgettes with orange, place 750 g (1½ lb) sliced courgettes and the grated rind and juice of 2 oranges in a saucepan. Cover tightly and simmer for about 4 minutes until the courgettes are tender. Add 25 g (1 oz) butter, season with pepper and toss until the courgettes are well coated.

braised red cabbage

Serves **8**
Preparation time **15 minutes**
Cooking time **2¼ hours**

1 head **red cabbage**, about
   1.5 kg (3 lb), finely shredded
50 g (2 oz) **fat salt pork**,
   diced, or **butter**
2 **Spanish onions**, thinly
   sliced
4 tablespoons **brown sugar**
250 g (8 oz) **tart dessert
   apples**, peeled, cored and
   chopped
150 ml (¼ pint) **chicken stock**
150 ml (¼ pint) **red wine**
3 tablespoons **wine vinegar**
   or **cider vinegar**
1 small **raw beetroot**, coarsely
   grated
salt and **pepper**

Put the cabbage in a large bowl. Cover with boiling water and set aside.

Using a large heavy-based pan, either sauté the pork until the fat runs or melt the butter. Add the onions and fry, stirring frequently, over a moderate heat until soft and transparent. Stir in the sugar and continue to fry gently until the onions are caramelized and a rich golden colour. Take great care not to let the sugar burn.

Drain the cabbage thoroughly. Add it to the pan with the apples, stock, wine and vinegar. Mix well. Season generously with salt and pepper. Cover tightly and cook gently for 1½ hours, stirring occasionally.

Mix in the grated beetroot – this transforms the colour – and continue to cook, covered, for 30 minutes longer, or until the cabbage is soft. Adjust the seasoning, if necessary, and serve very hot.

For crunchy red cabbage, proceed as above, adding 125 g (4 oz) sultanas at the same time as you add the apples. Just before serving, stir 125 g (4 oz) blanched whole almonds into the red cabbage.

roast sweet potatoes

Serves **6**
Preparation time **6 minutes**
Cooking time **50 minutes**

1 kg (2 lb) **sweet potatoes**,
    peeled and cut into even-
    sized pieces
50 g (2 oz) **butter**
1 tablespoon **oil**
1 tablespoon **clear honey**
pinch of **ground ginger**
salt and **pepper**

Drop the sweet potatoes into a saucepan of salted boiling water and simmer for 5 minutes, then drain.

Melt half the butter with the oil in a flameproof dish and stir in the honey and ginger. Add the sweet potatoes and toss in the honey mixture. Dot with the remaining butter, then season with salt and pepper.

Cook in a preheated oven, 180°C (350°F), Gas Mark 4, for 40 minutes, or until the potatoes are tender. Brush with the glaze in the pan and turn occasionally during cooking.

For honey-roast root vegetables, cut 500 g (1 lb) carrots, 500 g (1 lb) parsnips and 500 g (1 lb) turnips into 1 cm (½ inch) cubes. Heat 1 tablespoon oil in a frying pan and quickly fry the vegetables until just coloured. Transfer to a roasting tin, drizzle over 2 tablespoons clear honey, toss to coat evenly and roast in a preheated oven, 200°C (400°F), Gas Mark 6, for 1–1¼ hours, tossing frequently during cooking, until tender and well glazed.

onions stuffed with apple & stilton

Serves **4**
Preparation time **10 minutes**
Cooking time **50–55 minutes**

4 large **onions**, about 250 g
(8 oz) each
125 g (4 oz) **cooking apples**,
peeled, cored and chopped
50 g (2 oz) **fresh**
breadcrumbs
50 g (2 oz) **blue Stilton**
cheese, finely crumbled
½ bunch of **watercress**,
trimmed and finely chopped
50 g (2 oz) **butter**
salt and **pepper**

Cook the onions in boiling water for 15 minutes, until they are just tender. Drain and allow to cool until they can be handled.

Mix the apples with the breadcrumbs and cheese, then stir in the chopped watercress.

Remove the middle of each onion – this is easiest if you gradually scoop out the layers of onion with a teaspoon. Leave an unbroken shell about 2 layers thick. Chop the scooped-out onion from 1 of the onions (discarding the rest) and add to the cheese mixture. Mix well and season to taste, then press the mixture into the onion shells.

Stand the onions in an ovenproof dish and dot them with the butter. Bake in a preheated oven, 180°C (350°F), Gas Mark 4, for 35–40 minutes, or until the stuffing is cooked through.

For roast onions in their skins, slice the stem ends from 4 unpeeled onions, scrape the root ends and make a shallow cross in the core with a knife. Place the onions in a greased roasting tin and cook in a preheated oven, 200°C (400°F), Gas Mark 6, for about 1 hour, or until tender but still firm when pierced with a skewer. Remove from the oven, slip off the outer skins and place on a warmed serving dish. Season with salt and pepper. Squeeze slightly to open the centres and push a knob of butter into each onion. Garnish with watercress or parsley sprigs.

camembert leeks

Serves **4**
Preparation time **15 minutes**
Cooking time **18–20 minutes**

750 g (1½ lb) **baby leeks**
20 g (¾ oz) **butter**
½ tablespoon finely chopped
  onion
15 g (½ oz) **plain flour**
150 ml (¼ pint) **milk**
50 g (2 oz) **Camembert**
  cheese, rind removed,
  chopped
salt and **pepper**
chopped **parsley**, to garnish

Cook the leeks in boiling salted water for 8 minutes, or until tender. Drain and place in a shallow heatproof dish. Keep warm.

Melt the butter in a pan, add the onion and fry until soft. Stir in the flour and cook for 1 minute. Gradually blend in the milk. Heat, stirring, until the sauce thickens.

Add the Camembert and heat gently, stirring, until it has melted. Season to taste, then pour the sauce over the leeks. Garnish with parsley and serve immediately.

For cauliflower with Stilton, cook the florets of 1 cauliflower in boiling salted water for about 10 minutes or until tender. Drain and transfer to a warmed ovenproof serving dish. Make the cheese sauce as above, omitting the onion and replacing the Camembert with 75 g (3 oz) crumbled blue Stilton. Pour the sauce over the cauliflower and top with 2 tablespoons wholemeal breadcrumbs. Cook under a preheated medium grill until golden brown.

cold baked ham

Serves **10–12**
Preparation time **5 minutes**,
  plus soaking
Cooking time **2 hours
  25 minutes–3 hours**

2.5–4 kg (5½–8½ lb) **gammon
  joint**, either on the bone or
  boned and rolled
2 **bay leaves**
8 tablespoons **demerara
  sugar**
3 tablespoons **ginger
  marmalade**
150 ml (¼ pint) **ginger ale**

Place the gammon in a large saucepan of cold water
and leave to soak for 2–12 hours depending on the
amount of salt in the cure (soak overnight if in doubt).

Drain the gammon, then weigh it and calculate the
cooking time based on 25 minutes per 500 g (1 lb),
plus 20 minutes. For a joint over 3 kg (6½ lb), allow
20 minutes per 500 g (1 lb), plus 20 minutes. Return
it to the pan and cover with fresh cold water. Add the
bay leaves and 2 tablespoons of the sugar and bring to
the boil. Cover, reduce the heat and simmer for half the
calculated cooking time.

Remove the gammon from the water and strip off
the skin. Stand the joint on a large sheet of foil in a
roasting tin and score the fat diagonally in a trellis
pattern. Mix the marmalade and remaining sugar and
spread over the fat. Pour the ginger ale around the joint
and enclose in the foil, sealing the edges firmly.

Bake in a preheated oven, 190°C (375°F), Gas Mark
5, for the remaining cooking time. During cooking,
baste the gammon with the ginger ale, then rewrap
in the foil. About 20 minutes before the end of the
cooking time, fold back the foil, baste again and return
to the oven. Remove and leave to cool overnight.

For cranberry baked ham, use 3 tablespoons ready-
made cranberry and orange sauce instead of the
marmalade. Omit the ginger ale and pour 150 ml
(¼ pint) dry cider around the joint.

festive game pie

Serves **8**

Preparation time **45 minutes**, plus cooling

Cooking time 1½ **hours**

450 g (14½ oz) **sausagemeat**

2 **onions**, finely chopped

2 teaspoons chopped **thyme**

75 g (3 oz) **butter**

400 g (13 oz) lean **turkey**, diced

4 **pigeon breasts**, sliced

500 g (1 lb) **pheasant**, diced

2 **celery sticks**, thinly sliced

3 **garlic cloves**, crushed

3 tablespoons **plain flour**

900 ml (1½ pints) **game** or **chicken stock**

200 g (7 oz) vacuum-packed cooked, peeled **chestnuts**, halved

milk, to glaze

salt and **pepper**

Shortcrust pastry

375 g (12 oz) **plain flour**

125 g (4 oz) **butter**, diced

125 g (4 oz) **lard**, diced

2 teaspoons iced **water**

pinch of **salt**

Place the flour and salt in a bowl, add the fats and rub in with the fingertips until the mixture resembles coarse breadcrumbs. Use a round-bladed knife to stir in the measured water until the mixture starts to bind. Bring to a dough, adding a little more water if it feels dry. Lightly knead on a floured surface until smooth. Wrap and chill until required.

Combine the sausagemeat with 1 chopped onion and a little thyme and shape into 18 small balls. Melt 25 g (1 oz) of the butter in a frying pan, fry the meatballs until golden, then drain. Season all the other meats and fry, in batches, until golden, adding more butter if needed. Drain.

Melt the rest of the butter in the pan and fry the remaining onion and the celery and garlic. Blend in the flour, add the stock and bring to the boil. Cook for 4–5 minutes.

Mix all the meats and chestnuts in a 2 litre (3½ pint) pie dish and pour over enough of the liquid to come to within 2 cm (¾ inch) of the rim. Leave to cool.

Roll out the pastry on a lightly floured surface until 5 cm (2 inches) larger than the pie dish. Cut a 2.5 cm (1 inch) strip from around the edges and place it on the dampened rim of the dish. Brush with milk, cover with the pastry lid, fluting the edges with the back of a knife, and score a cross in the centre. Use the pastry trimmings to make leaves for the top, then brush with more milk. Bake in a preheated oven, 190°C (375°F), Gas Mark 5, for 1 hour, until deep golden, covering with foil if the pastry begins to get too brown.

chicken liver pâté

Serves **4–6**
Preparation time **20 minutes**,
  plus cooling and chilling
Cooking time **10 minutes**

375 g (12 oz) **unsalted butter**
2 **garlic cloves**, crushed
500 g (1 lb) **chicken livers**,
  cores removed, roughly
  chopped
6–8 tablespoons **brandy**,
  according to taste
salt and **pepper**

Melt 50 g (2 oz) of the butter in a large frying pan over moderate heat until foaming. Reduce the heat, add the garlic and stir for 2–3 minutes until it is softened but not coloured.

Add the chicken livers, increase the heat to moderate and toss vigorously for 5–8 minutes until the livers are browned on the outside, but still remain pink-tinged in the centre.

Pour in the brandy and stir well. Let the mixture bubble for 1–2 minutes, then transfer to a food processor or blender. Cut all but 50 g (2 oz) of the remaining butter into pieces and add to the machine. Work the mixture to a smooth pureé and season to taste.

Turn the mixture into individual ramekins or a large serving bowl and smooth the surface. Melt the remaining butter in a clean pan, then pour over the surface of the pâté. Leave until cold, then cover and chill overnight in the refrigerator. Serve the pâté chilled, accompanied by triangles of hot wholemeal toast, if liked.

For Stilton & walnut pâté, melt 25 g (1 oz) butter in a pan, add 25 g (1 oz) flour and cook for 1 minute. Gradually add 200 ml (7 fl oz) milk, mixing well, then bring to the boil, stirring constantly, and cook until smooth and thickened. Remove from the heat, crumble in 125 g (4 oz) blue Stilton and stir until melted. Add 50 g (2 oz) chopped walnuts and 2 teaspoons each chopped parsley and brandy, and season. Serve chilled, garnished with some walnut pieces and small parsley sprigs.

winter salad

Serves **8**

Preparation time **20 minutes**

2 **green-skinned dessert apples**, cored and sliced

2 **red-skinned dessert apples**, cored and sliced

2 **conference pears**, peeled, cored and sliced

2 tablespoons **lemon juice**

1 head **celery**, sliced

50–75 g (2–3 oz) **shelled walnuts**

4 **spring onions**, finely sliced

100 g (3½ oz) **watercress**

5 tablespoons **French dressing**

Place the apples, pears and lemon juice in a large bowl. Stir lightly but thoroughly to mix, then pour off the excess lemon juice.

Add the celery, walnuts, spring onions and watercress.

Pour the French dressing over the salad. Toss lightly but thoroughly, then turn into a salad bowl, cover and chill in the refrigerator until required.

For spinach & Roquefort salad, place 375 g (12 oz) trimmed baby spinach leaves and 75 g (3 oz) roughly chopped walnuts in a salad bowl. To make the dressing, use a fork to mash 50 g (2 oz) Roquefort cheese with 150 ml (¼ pint) half-fat crème fraîche and a little milk until smooth. Add the mashed mixture to the salad bowl, toss the ingredients thoroughly and serve at once.

roast vegetable & bread salad

Serves **4**

Preparation time **25 minutes**, plus cooling

Cooking time **50 minutes**

1 large **aubergine**, cubed

4 **courgettes**, cubed

2 **red peppers**, cored, deseeded and sliced

4 **garlic cloves**

about 4 tablespoons **extra virgin olive oil**

4 firm ripe **tomatoes**, diced

175 g (6 oz) day-old **bread**, diced

2 tablespoons boiling **water**

handful of small **basil leaves**

salt and **pepper**

Dressing

9 tablespoons **extra virgin olive oil**

2 tablespoons **red wine vinegar**

pinch of **sugar**

Toss the aubergine, courgettes, peppers and garlic with the olive oil and place in a large roasting tin. Bake in a preheated oven, 220°C (425°F), Gas Mark 7, for 50 minutes. Remove the tin from the oven and stir in the tomatoes, adding a little extra oil if necessary.

Whisk together the oil, vinegar, sugar and a little seasoning. Stir 3 tablespoons of the dressing into the vegetables and leave to cool.

Place the bread in a bowl. Add the measured boiling water to the remaining dressing and stir into the bread, then leave to soak for 10 minutes.

Add the bread to the vegetables with the basil and season to taste before serving.

For pancetta & flageolet bean salad, lightly fry 125 g (4 oz) pancetta cubes in a nonstick frying pan for 2–3 minutes, turning occasionally. When cooked, tip the pancetta and cooking juices into a bowl containing 2 x 400 g (13 oz) cans flageolet beans, drained, and 4 chopped spring onions. Toss well, season to taste and serve warm or cold.

traditional christmas pudding

Serves **12**
Preparation time **30 minutes**
Cooking time **9–12 hours**

125 g (4 oz) **self-raising flour**
175 g (6 oz) **fresh white breadcrumbs**
175 g (6 oz) **currants**
175 g (6 oz) **sultanas**
125 g (4 oz) **pitted dates**, chopped
250 g (8 oz) **pitted raisins**
175 g (6 oz) **shredded suet**
50 g (2 oz) **cut mixed peel**
50 g (2 oz) **blanched almonds**, chopped
1 small **apple**, peeled, cored and grated
grated rind and juice of 1 small **orange**
½ teaspoon **ground mixed spice**
¼ teaspoon grated **nutmeg**
½ teaspoon **salt**
3 **eggs**
4 tablespoons **brown ale** or **cider**
250 g (8 oz) **soft dark brown sugar**
3–4 tablespoons **brandy**, to serve

Place all the pudding ingredients in a large bowl and stir well to mix.

Grease liberally a 1.2 litre (2 pint) pudding basin and a 600 ml (1 pint) pudding basin. Spoon the mixture into each basin until just over three-quarters full, then cover with circles of greased greaseproof paper, then with foil or a pudding cloth. Fold a pleat in the centre and tie string securely around the rim.

Place in the top of a steamer or double boiler, or put in a large pan and pour in boiling water to come halfway up the sides. Boil for 6–8 hours, depending on size, topping up with boiling water as necessary. Remove the puddings from the pans and leave overnight to cool.

Remove the coverings and recover with fresh greased greaseproof paper and foil or a pudding cloth. Store in a cool, dry, dark place for up to 6 months.

Reboil the puddings for 3–4 hours, depending on size, then turn out on to a warm dish. Warm the brandy, pour over the pudding and set alight. Serve with crème anglaise (see below) or brandy butter, rum butter or brandy cream (see page 84).

For crème anglaise, to serve 6, heat 300 ml (½ pint) milk with 300 ml (½ pint) single cream in a heavy-based pan and bring slowly to the boil. Whisk 6 egg yolks and 25 g (1 oz) caster sugar in a bowl until thick and pale, then add 2 teaspoons vanilla extract. Pour the milk and cream mixture over the yolk and sugar mixture, whisking well. Cook over a moderate heat for 5–10 minutes, stirring constantly, until the sauce thickly coats the back of the spoon. Serve warm.

last-minute christmas pudding

Serves **8**
Preparation time
30 minutes, plus standing
Cooking time **6–7 hours**

125 g (4 oz) **dark molasses
sugar**
200 g (7 oz) **fresh white
breadcrumbs**
125 g (4 oz) **shredded suet**
pinch of **salt**
1 teaspoon **ground mixed
spice**
175 g (6 oz) **sultanas**
175 g (6 oz) **pitted raisins**
125 g (4 oz) **currants**
50 g (2 oz) **candied peel**,
chopped
25 g (1 oz) **blanched
almonds**, finely chopped
1 large **cooking apple**,
peeled, cored and finely
chopped
finely grated rind and juice of
½ **lemon**
1 **egg**, beaten
150 ml (¼ pint) **Guinness** or
milk stout
about 75 ml (3 fl oz) **milk**
icing sugar, for dusting
2 tablespoons **brandy**,
to serve

Put the dry ingredients, dried fruit, candied peel and almonds into a large bowl and stir well to mix. Add the apple with the lemon rind and juice, egg and Guinness or milk stout and stir well. Add enough milk to make a soft dropping consistency.

Turn into a greased 1.2 litre (2 pint) pudding basin. Cover the top of the pudding with a circle of greased greaseproof paper, then with foil, or tie up the basin in a pudding cloth. Fold a pleat in the centre and tie string around the rim. Leave to stand overnight.

Place the basin in the top of a steamer or double boiler, or in a large pan of gently bubbling water, and steam for 4–5 hours, topping up with more boiling water as necessary.

Remove the basin carefully from the pan and leave to cool completely. Discard the foil and greaseproof paper. Replace with fresh greaseproof paper and foil if you intend to store the pudding, but it doesn't need to mature and can be made just before Christmas.

Steam again for 2 hours before serving. Dust with icing sugar and decorate with a holly leaf, if liked. Warm the brandy, pour over the pudding and set alight. Serve with crème anglaise (see page 80) or brandy butter, rum butter or brandy cream (see page 84).

For individual Christmas puddings, make the pudding mixture as described above and use to fill 8 individual 150 ml (¼ pint) pudding tins. Cover as above, then steam for just 2 hours. Steam again for about 1 hour before serving.

brandy butter

Serves **6**
Preparation time
10–15 minutes

175 g (6 oz) **unsalted butter**,
softened
175 g (6 oz) **icing sugar**,
sifted
thinly grated rind of ½ **orange**,
plus a few thinly pared strips
to garnish
2 tablespoons **brandy**

Put the butter in a bowl and, using an electric or hand-held rotary whisk, beat until light and fluffy. Gradually beat in the icing sugar, then beat in the orange rind and the brandy.

Turn the brandy butter into a serving bowl and chill in the refrigerator until quite firm. Serve garnished with thinly pared strips of orange rind.

For rum butter, beat the butter as above, using 125 g (4 oz) unsalted softened butter, 50 g (2 oz) soft brown sugar and 25 ml (1 fl oz) light rum.

For brandy cream, whip 300 ml (½ pint) whipping cream with 1 tablespoon icing sugar, using an electric or hand-held rotary whisk, until soft peaks form. Add 2 tablespoons brandy (or Cointreau, if preferred) and stir to combine.

bombe noël

Serves **6–8**
Preparation time **20 minutes**,
  plus soaking and freezing
Cooking time **10 minutes**

125 g (4 oz) **glacé cherries**,
  chopped, plus extra whole
  ones to decorate (optional)
50 g (2 oz) **dried cranberries**,
  chopped
50 g (2 oz) **crystallized
  pineapple**, chopped
50 g (2 oz) **preserved stem
  ginger**, drained and
  chopped
75 g (3 oz) **seedless raisins**
4 tablespoons **brandy**
3 **egg yolks**
75 g (3 oz) **caster sugar**
300 ml (½ pint) **single cream**
150 ml (¼ pint) **double cream**
6 tablespoons chopped
  toasted **almonds**, plus extra
  whole ones to decorate
  (optional)
crystallized ginger, chopped,
  to decorate (optional)

Place the cherries, cranberries, pineapple, ginger and raisins in a bowl. Pour the brandy over and leave to soak for 1 hour.

Beat the yolks and sugar until thoroughly combined. Bring the single cream just to the boil, remove from the heat and stir gradually into the yolk mix. Transfer to a heatproof bowl over a pan of simmering water and cook gently, stirring constantly, until the custard is thick enough to coat the back of a spoon. Strain into a bowl and leave to cool, stirring occasionally.

Whip the double cream until it stands in soft peaks, then fold in the cold custard. Freeze in a rigid container, covered, for 2–3 hours until half-frozen. Stir in the fruit, brandy and chopped almonds. Place in a 1 litre (1¾ pint) foil pudding bowl and level the surface.

Cover the bowl with foil, then wrap in a polythene bag. Seal and freeze for up to 3 months. To defrost and serve, unwrap the bowl and invert on to a serving plate. Rub with a cloth wrung out in very hot water until the bombe drops out. Place in the refrigerator for 30 minutes. Decorate with some whole glacé cherries and toasted almonds and a few pieces of chopped crystallized ginger, if liked.

For Christmas pudding ice cream, replace the glacé cherries, cranberries, crystallized pineapple, ginger and raisins with 400 g (13 oz) dried mixed luxury fruit. Add 1 teaspoon each ground mixed spice and ground cinnamon to the frozen cream and custard mixture with the brandy-soaked fruit and the almonds. Omit the glacé cherry, toasted almond and ginger decoration.

ricotta & candied fruit slice

Serves **8**
Preparation time **20 minutes**
Cooking time **25 minutes**

350 g (12 oz) **ready-made puff pastry**, defrosted if frozen
a little **flour**, for dusting
icing sugar, for dusting

Filling
250 g (8 oz) **firm ricotta cheese**
75 g (3 oz) **mixed candied fruit**, finely chopped
50 g (2 oz) **plain dark chocolate**, finely chopped
grated rind of 1 **lemon**
beaten **egg**, to glaze
25 g (1 oz) **flaked almonds**

Roll out the pastry on a lightly floured surface until it is 2.5 mm (⅛ inch) thick and a 20 x 30 cm (8 x 12 inch) rectangle. Place the rectangle on a baking sheet lined with baking paper.

Make the filling. Beat the ricotta until it is smooth and then stir in the candied fruit, chocolate and lemon rind. Spread the mixture down the centre of the pastry, leaving a 5 cm (2 inch) border down each side.

Score the pastry lightly along each side of the filling and fold over the pastry sides to cover the edges of the filling. Brush the pastry with beaten egg and sprinkle over the flaked almonds, pressing them down lightly.

Bake in a preheated oven, 200°C (400°F), Gas Mark 6, for 25 minutes until risen and golden, then remove from the oven and leave to cool.

Dust the tart generously with icing sugar before serving cut in slices.

For ricotta & date slice, omit the candied fruit and lemon rind and stir 175 g (3 oz) chopped pitted dates and the grated rind of 1 orange into the cheese, together with the chocolate. Continue as above.

clementine & mincemeat tart

Serves **6**
Preparation time **20 minutes**,
  plus chilling
Cooking time **33–40 minutes**

75 g (3 oz) **plain flour**
75 g (3 oz) **wholemeal flour**
75 g (3 oz) chilled **butter**,
  diced
50 g (2 oz) **ground almonds**
25 g (1 oz) **caster sugar**
grated rind of **1 orange**
1 **egg**, beaten
375 g (12 oz) **luxury**
  mincemeat
3 **clementines**, segmented
milk, to glaze
icing sugar, for dusting

Put both the flours in a bowl, add the butter and rub in with the fingertips until the mixture resembles fine breadcrumbs. Stir in the almonds, sugar and orange rind, then add the egg and mix to a firm dough.

Knead the dough briefly on a lightly floured surface, then roll out and use to line a 23 cm (9 inch) loose-bottomed fluted flan tin. Prick the base with a fork, chill for 15 minutes, then line with nonstick baking paper and add macaroni or baking beans. Bake blind in a preheated oven, 190°C (375°F), Gas Mark 5, for 10–15 minutes. Remove the paper and macaroni or beans and return to the oven for a further 5 minutes.

Mix the mincemeat and clementine segments, then fill the pastry case. Gather up the pastry trimmings, re-roll and cut into differently sized stars. Place on the topping, brush with milk and dust with icing sugar.

Bake at the above temperature for 18–20 minutes until the fruit is caramelized and the stars look baked. Dust with icing sugar and serve warm or cold.

For cranberry & mincemeat latticed tart, bake the pastry case as above. Fill with the mincemeat mixed with 175 g (6 oz) fresh or frozen cranberries instead of the clementines. Re-roll the pastry trimmings thinly and cut into 1 cm (½ in) wide strips. Dampen the edges of the pastry case and, twisting it slightly, lay a pastry strip across one side of the tart, pressing the edges to seal. Lay a second twisted strip of pastry at right angles to the first. Continue attaching twisted pastry strips alternately at right angles. Trim off excess pastry and cook as above.

frosted grapes

Serves **6–8**

Preparation time **20 minutes**, plus setting

½ bunch of **green seedless grapes**

½ bunch of **red seedless grapes**

a few **physalis** (optional), with some leaves left intact

125 g (4 oz) **icing sugar**

4–5 teaspoons **orange** or **lime juice**

50 g (2 oz) **caster sugar**

Wash the grapes and the physalis (if using), then pat dry with kitchen paper. Snip the grapes into tiny bunches of 2–3 grapes.

Sift the icing sugar into a bowl, then gradually mix in the fruit juice to make a smooth, thick frosting.

Dip the grapes a bunch at a time into the frosting, then dip the physalis. Arrange the grapes and physalis on a wire rack set over a baking sheet. Leave in a cool place for 1 hour or until hardened.

Sprinkle the grapes and physalis with caster sugar before serving.

For crystallized fruits, use a selection of fruits with edible skins, for example small bunches of grapes or redcurrants, or strawberries, plums and pears. Brush lightly with beaten egg white and place in a colander set over a large bowl. Sprinkle the fruit generously with granulated sugar and leave to stand until the sugar has hardened.

winter dried fruit salad

Serves **6**
Preparation time **5 minutes**,
  plus soaking
Cooking time **10–15 minutes**

175 g (6 oz) **dried apricots**
125 g (4 oz) **dried prunes**
125 g (4 oz) **dried figs**
125 g (4 oz) **dried apples**
600 ml (1 pint) **apple juice**
2 tablespoons **Calvados** or
  brandy
25 g (1 oz) **walnuts**, roughly
  chopped

Place the dried fruits in a bowl with the apple juice and leave to soak overnight.

Transfer the fruits and juice to a saucepan and simmer for 10–15 minutes.

Turn into a glass bowl and pour over the Calvados or brandy. Sprinkle with the walnuts. Serve warm or cold with crème fraîche or cream.

For fruit & nut crumble, soak and simmer the dried fruits as above, then turn into an ovenproof dish. Omit the Calvados or brandy and walnuts and make a crumble topping instead. Rub 75 g (3 oz) unsalted butter into 175 g (6 oz) wholemeal flour until the mixture resembles breadcrumbs. Stir in 50 g (2 oz) soft dark brown sugar and 50 g (2 oz) chopped hazelnuts. Sprinkle over the fruit mixture and bake in a preheated oven 200°C (400°F), Gas Mark 6, for 25–30 minutes.

poached pears in cassis

Serves **6**
Preparation time **10 minutes**
Cooking time **50 minutes**

300 ml (½ pint) **red wine**
150 ml (¼ pint) **cassis**
2 **cinnamon sticks**
2 strips **lemon rind**
2 strips **orange rind**
300 ml (½ pint) **water**
6 firm, ripe **pears**, peeled
150 g (5 oz) **Greek yogurt**
2 tablespoons **Greek honey**
1 teaspoon **ground cinnamon**

Place the wine, cassis, cinnamon sticks, citrus peel and measured water in a saucepan and bring to the boil. Add the pears, cover the pan and simmer gently for about 40 minutes until the pears are cooked through but not mushy.

Remove the pears with a slotted spoon and place in a serving dish. Bring the poaching liquid to a rolling boil and simmer until it is reduced by half and is thick and syrupy. Pour over the pears and leave to cool.

Combine the yogurt, honey and cinnamon and set aside to allow the flavours to develop. Serve the pears at room temperature with a spoonful of the cinnamon cream for each serving.

For poached figs, replace the pears with 12 large, firm, ripe figs. Cook the figs in the syrup as above for 10 minutes until they are dark red and softened (don't overcook or the figs will fall apart). Remove the figs from the syrup and continue as above. This recipe serves 4.

ginger & hazelnut ice cream

Serves **4**

Preparation time **5 minutes**,
plus freezing

300 ml (½ pint) **double cream**

2 tablespoons **milk**

4 tablespoons **icing sugar**,
sifted

50 g (2 oz) **preserved stem
ginger**, drained and finely
chopped

4 teaspoons **ginger syrup**

2–4 tablespoons finely
chopped **hazelnuts**, plus
extra to decorate

Whip the cream and milk lightly, then fold in the icing
sugar. Pour into a shallow freezer container, cover and
freeze for about 45 minutes, until the ice cream has
frozen around the sides of the container.

Turn into a chilled bowl and whisk until smooth. Stir in
the ginger, syrup and hazelnuts.

Return the ice cream to the container, cover and
freeze until firm. Transfer to the refrigerator about
20 minutes before serving, to soften.

Scoop into dishes and sprinkle with a few extra
chopped hazelnuts to serve.

For maple & pecan ice cream, omit the preserved
ginger, ginger syrup and hazelnuts, and stir in 75 g
(3 oz) finely chopped pecans and 4 teaspoons pure
maple syrup instead. Continue as above.

champagne strawberry cup

Serves **6**
Preparation time **5 minutes**

175 ml (6 fl oz) **strawberry liqueur** (such as fraises des bois), chilled
1 bottle non-vintage **dry Champagne** or **dry sparkling white wine**, chilled
125 g (4 oz) **strawberries**, sliced

Pour the liqueur into a large jug. Gradually add the Champagne or sparkling wine, stirring very gently so as not to lose the bubbles.

Divide the strawberry slices among individual Champagne flutes and top up with the strawberry-flavoured Champagne. Serve at once.

For kir royale, pour chilled dry Champagne or sparkling white wine into Champagne flutes. Slowly add 25 ml (1 fl oz) crème de cassis to each glass so that it gently mingles with the Champagne to give a pale pink glass of fizz.

For classic Champagne cocktail, place a sugar cube in each Champagne flute. Saturate it with Angostura bitters, then add 25 ml (1 fl oz) brandy to each glass. Top with chilled Champagne.

glühwein

Serves **6**
Preparation time **5 minutes**
Cooking time **10–12 minutes**

2 **lemons**, sliced
1 **orange**, sliced
1 bottle **red wine**
125 g (4 oz) **sugar**
8 whole **cloves**
2 **cinnamon sticks**
150 ml (¼ pint) **brandy**

Place the slices of 1 lemon in a saucepan with the sliced orange, red wine, sugar, cloves and cinnamon sticks. Simmer gently for 10 minutes, then reduce the heat and add the brandy.

Serve the glühwein in small cups or heatproof glasses with the remaining slices of lemon.

For party glögg, to serve 15–20, place the rind of 1 orange, 20 lightly crushed cardamom pods, 20 whole cloves and 2 cinnamon sticks in a piece of muslin, tie securely and add to a saucepan with 1 bottle red wine, 1 bottle port or Madeira, 175 g (6 oz) blanched almonds and 250 g (8 oz) raisins. Heat at just below boiling point for 25 minutes, stirring occasionally. Place 250–375 g (8–12 oz) sugar cubes on a wire rack over the pan. Warm 300 ml (½ pint) brandy and pour evenly over the sugar cubes. Set the cubes alight: they will melt through the wire rack into the wine. Stir the glögg and remove the spice bag. Serve hot, with a few raisins and almonds in each cup.

centrepiece cakes

rich christmas cake

Serves **16**
Preparation time **45 minutes**,
  plus cooling
Cooking time **3–3½ hours**

125 g (4 oz) **self-raising flour**
200 g (7 oz) **plain flour**
¼ teaspoon **salt**
1 teaspoon **ground mixed
  spice**
½ teaspoon **ground cinnamon**
½ teaspoon **ground nutmeg**
250 g (8 oz) **butter**
250 g (8 oz) **soft dark brown**
  or **dark muscovado sugar**
2 teaspoons **black treacle**
5 **eggs**
50 ml (2 fl oz) **medium-dry
  sherry** or strained cold **tea**
1½ teaspoons **vanilla extract**
250 g (8 oz) **currants**
250 g (8 oz) **sultanas**
250 g (8 oz) **prunes** or **dates**,
  roughly chopped
250 g (8 oz) **seedless raisins**
75 g (3 oz) **cut mixed peel**
50 g (2 oz) **ground almonds**
75 g (3 oz) **glacé cherries**,
  halved
finely grated rind of 1 **lemon**
3–4 tablespoons **brandy**

Grease and line a 23 cm (9 inch) round or 20 cm (8 inch) square cake tin, using a double thickness of greased greaseproof paper. Line the outside with several thicknesses of brown paper, standing at least 5 cm (2 inches) above the top of the tin.

Sift the flours into a bowl with the salt, mixed spice, cinnamon and nutmeg. In another large bowl, cream the butter with the sugar until light. Beat in the treacle.

Lightly beat together the eggs, sherry or tea and vanilla extract. Gradually beat half the egg mixture into the creamed mixture. Fold in one-third of the mixed flours. Continue to add the egg and flour mixtures alternately. Mix in all the remaining ingredients except the brandy. Turn into the prepared tin and smooth the top.

Bake in a preheated oven, 140°C (275°F), Gas Mark 1, for about 3–3½ hours until a skewer inserted into the centre of the cake comes out clean. Cover the cake with a double layer of greaseproof paper if it starts to brown too much during cooking.

Leave the cake to cool in the tin before turning out on to a wire rack to cool completely. Prick all over with a fine skewer and spoon brandy over the cake. Store the cake in an airtight tin and leave to mature for about 1 month before using.

For iced rich Christmas cake, brush the cake all over with smooth apricot jam, then cover with 1 kg (2 lb) marzipan (use half this quantity if you want to cover only the top of the cake). Ice the whole cake with 2–3 coats of thin royal icing (see page 10).

santa's sack

Serves **10**

Preparation time **25 minutes**

18 x 10 cm (7 x 4 inch)
  ready-made rich fruit cake
2 tablespoons **smooth**
  apricot jam
750 g (1½ lb) **red ready-to-**
  roll icing
selection of **wrapped**
  chocolates and **chocolate**
  coins
75 g (3 oz) **white ready-to-**
  roll icing

Put the cake on a serving plate or cake board and spread the sides with the apricot jam, reserving a little.

Knead the red icing until softened, then roll out thinly on a surface lightly dusted with icing sugar. Cut out 2 rectangles, 19 x 16 cm (7½ x 6½ inches), and press them on to the long sides of the cake. Re-roll the trimmings and cut out 2 x 13 cm (5½ inch) squares. Press them on to the short ends of the cake.

Smooth the icing over the cake and press the icing joins together. Don't worry if the icing sags down the sides – this will make the sack look more interesting. Smooth the top edge of the icing to give a wavy effect, then fill the top of the sack with sweets and coins. Roll out the white icing and stamp out tiny stars or holly leaves. Stick them on to the sides of the sack with a little jam.

For Madeira cake Santa's sack, use 2 x 275 g (9 oz) ready-made Madeira cake bars instead of the fruit cake. Sandwich the long edges together with jam or Vanilla Butter Icing (see page 120), then ice and decorate as above.

christmas wreath cake

Serves **16**

Preparation time **1 hour**

1 x 23 cm (9 inch) **Rich Christmas Cake** (see page 106)

4 tablespoons **smooth apricot jam**

1 kg (2 lb) **white marzipan**

1 kg (2 lb) **white ready-to-roll icing**

red, **dark green**, **citrus green** and **light green food colourings**

75 g (3 oz) **plain dark chocolate**, broken into pieces

Brush the cake with 3 tablespoons apricot jam. Set aside 175 g (6 oz) marzipan and use the rest to cover the cake, smoothing it over the top and down the sides. Trim to fit. Place the cake on a cake board.

Knead the icing lightly and roll out on a work surface dusted with icing sugar until large enough to cover the cake. Dampen the marzipan, then lift the icing carefully over the cake, supporting it with a rolling pin. Smooth over the top, then down the sides. Trim off the excess icing. Colour icing trimmings with red food colouring to make holly berries. Leave to dry on baking paper.

Wrap a rolling pin with nonstick baking paper. Melt the chocolate in a heatproof bowl over a pan of gently simmering water. Drizzle the melted chocolate quickly back and forth across the rolling pin. Allow to set.

Divide the reserved marzipan into 3, colour each third a different shade of green and place in plastic bags to prevent drying out. Lightly knead two green shades together to give a marbled effect. Roll out thinly on a surface lightly dusted with icing sugar and cut out ivy leaves. Mark with veins and twist slightly.

Roll out the remaining coloured marzipan and cut out light green and dark green holly leaves. Mark with veins and shape. Leave all the marzipan shapes to dry overnight on baking paper.

Use a dampened paintbrush to moisten the icing so you can attach the leaves and berries in a wreath shape. Peel the chocolate off the paper, break into 'twigs' and place on the wreath.

epiphany ring

Serves **12**

Preparation time **15–20 minutes**, plus rising

Cooking time **20–25 minutes**

500 g (1 lb) **strong white flour**

1 teaspoon **salt**

grated rind of 1 **orange**

grated rind of 1 **lemon**

125 g (4 oz) **caster sugar**

1½ teaspoons **fast-action dried yeast**

75 g (3 oz) **butter**, melted

2 **eggs**, beaten, plus extra **yolk** to glaze

175 ml (6 fl oz) **water**

100 g (3½ oz) **whole candied peel**

125 g (4 oz) **glacé cherries**

125 g (4 oz) **slivered blanched almonds**

1 tablespoon cold **water**

125 g (4 oz) **icing sugar**

4–5 teaspoons **lemon juice**

Put the flour in a large bowl, then stir in the salt, rinds, sugar and yeast. Add the butter and beaten eggs, then gradually mix in enough warm water to make a soft dough. Knead well until the dough is smooth and elastic. Put back into the bowl and cover with greased clingfilm. Leave in a warm place to rise for 1¼ hours or until doubled in size.

Tip out on to a lightly floured surface and knead well. Roughly chop the candied peel, cherries and almonds. Reserve one-third of the mixture, then gradually knead the remainder into the dough.

Shape into a thick rope 50 cm (20 inches) long and push the ends together to make a ring. Place on a greased baking sheet. Stand a greased bowl in the centre of the ring to keep the hole and cover loosely with greased clingfilm. Leave to rise for 30 minutes or until half as big again.

Remove the bowl, brush with yolk mixed with the water and bake in a preheated oven, 200°C (400°F), Gas Mark 6, for 20–25 minutes until the bread is golden brown and sounds hollow when tapped. Cover with foil if overbrowning. Transfer to a wire rack to cool.

Sift the icing sugar into a bowl, then gradually mix in the lemon juice to make a smooth, pouring icing. Drizzle over the bread in random lines. Sprinkle with the reserved fruit and nuts, then leave to set.

For epiphany ring with orange icing, replace 25–50 g (1–2 oz) of the glacé cherries with 25–50 g (1–2 oz) sultanas. Omit the lemon juice and instead mix 4–5 teaspoons orange juice with the icing sugar.

bûche de noël

Serves **10**
Preparation time **40 minutes**, plus cooling
Cooking time **20 minutes**

3 **eggs**
75 g (3 oz) **icing sugar**, plus extra for dusting
50 g (2 oz) **plain flour**
25 g (1 oz) **cocoa powder**
300 ml (½ pint) **double cream**
150 g (5 oz) canned **sweetened chestnut purée**
200 g (7 oz) **plain dark chocolate**, broken into pieces

Grease a 33 x 23 cm (13 x 9 inch) Swiss roll tin and line it with nonstick baking paper. Whisk the eggs and sugar in a heatproof bowl over a pan of hot water until the mixture leaves a trail when the whisk is lifted. Sift in the flour and cocoa powder and fold in.

Pour into the prepared tin and spread into the corners. Bake in a preheated oven, 180°C (350°F), Gas Mark 4, for about 15 minutes until just firm. Invert the cake on to a sheet of nonstick baking paper dusted with icing sugar. Peel away the paper that lined the tin, then roll the sponge in the fresh paper and leave to cool.

Whip half the cream until softly peaking, then fold in the chestnut purée. Unroll the sponge and spread the chestnut cream over the top (don't worry if the cake cracks). Roll the cake back into a log shape.

Bring the remainder of the cream almost to the boil. Remove from the heat and stir in the chocolate pieces. Leave until melted, then stir until smooth. Allow to cool.

Arrange the cake, seam side down, on a serving plate. Lightly whip the chocolate cream, then spread it over the top and sides of the cake, and mark to look like tree bark. Dust with icing sugar just before serving.

For brandy butter yule log, omit the chestnut filling and instead use 125 g (4 oz) brandy butter (see page 84) mixed with 150 ml (¼ pint) crème fraîche. Dust with cocoa powder instead of icing sugar. Mix 2 teaspoons arrowroot with 1 tablespoon cold water and add to 150 ml (¼ pint) warmed mulled wine. Heat the sauce until it is thickened and clear and serve with the yule log.

kids' twelfth night crown

Serves **8**

Preparation time **20 minutes**,
plus cooling

Cooking time **20–25 minutes**

175 g (6 oz) **unsalted butter**,
softened

175 g (6 oz) **caster sugar**

175 g (6 oz) **self-raising flour**

½ teaspoon **baking powder**

3 **eggs**

4 tablespoons **sugar strands**

500 g (1 lb) **yellow ready-to-
roll icing**

16 **black jelly beans**

1 tube **yellow writing icing**

9 **clear fruit sweets**

Kids' orange butter icing

75 g (3 oz) **unsalted butter**,
softened

200 g (7 oz) **icing sugar**,
sifted

1 teaspoon **orange juice**

2 teaspoons grated **orange
rind**

Beat the butter, caster sugar, self-raising flour, baking powder and eggs together until smooth. Grease 2 x 18 cm (7 inch) sandwich tins and line the bases with greased greaseproof paper. Spoon in the mixture and level the tops. Bake in a preheated oven, 180°C (350°F), Gas Mark 4, for 20–25 minutes. Turn out the cakes on to a wire rack and leave to cool.

Beat the butter, sugar and orange juice for the icing gradually together until light and fluffy, then stir in the rind. Use some of the icing to sandwich the cakes. Place on a cake board and spread butter icing thinly around the sides and thickly over the top. Sprinkle sugar strands over the top.

Knead the ready-to-roll icing until softened, then roll out on a surface lightly dusted with icing sugar. Trim to a 60 x 8 cm (24 x 3½ inch) rectangle. Scallop the top edge, using a plain 6 cm (2½ inch) biscuit cutter to cut semicircles out of the icing. Carefully press the strip of icing around the edge of the cake.

Knead the trimmings, shape into a 60 cm (24 inch) rope and stick around the base of the cake with a little butter icing. Trim the ends, if necessary. Spread the remaining butter icing over the icing rope to resemble a fur trim. Decorate with the jelly beans. Use plenty of writing icing to stick the fruit sweets on to the crown.

For kids' lemon crown cake, add the grated rind of 1 large lemon to the sponge ingredients. Omit the orange juice and rind from the butter icing and instead use 1 teaspoon lemon juice and 2 teaspoons grated lemon rind. Otherwise, prepare and bake as above.

gingerbread cottage

Serves **10**
Preparation time **1 hour**, plus
 chilling, cooling and setting
Cooking time **15–20 minutes**

175 g (6 oz) **clear honey**
65 g (2½ oz) **black treacle**
65 g (2½ oz) **unsalted butter**
625 g (1¼ lb) **plain flour**
1½ teaspoons **bicarbonate of
 soda**
1 tablespoon **ground ginger**
1 **egg**
2 **egg yolks**

To decorate
1 quantity **Royal Icing** (see
 page 10)
250 g (8 oz) **ready-to-roll
 icing**
**pink and white
 marshmallows**
selection of small **sweets**
 (such as dolly mixture)
icing sugar, for dusting

Heat the honey, treacle and butter in a pan until the
butter melts. Sift the flour, bicarbonate of soda and
ginger into a bowl. Add the egg and yolks to the
melted mixture, then pour over the dry ingredients and
mix to a dough. Wrap and chill for 30 minutes.

Roll out the dough on a floured surface and cut out
2 rectangles, 15 x 11 cm (6 x 4½ inches), for the roof.
Cut out 2 rectangles, 14 x 8 cm (5½ x 3½ inches), for
the sides and 2 squares, 14 cm (5½ inches), for the
ends. Trim each end piece into a triangle point running
from the centre of the top side to halfway down 2
opposite sides. Cut holes for doors and windows. From
the trimmings, make a door and 2 shutters per window.

Place on greased baking sheets. Bake in a preheated
oven, 180°C (350°F), Gas Mark 4, for 10–15 minutes
until colouring around the edges. Transfer to a wire
rack to cool.

Spoon royal icing into a piping bag with a writing
nozzle. Spread more icing over a silver cake board.
Secure the walls of the cottage to the board, gluing
sections together with icing. Spread the top edges with
icing and secure the roof. Leave for 2 hours to set.

Spread a little royal icing over the roof sections. Knead
and roll out the ready-to-roll icing and cover the roof.
Use icing trimmings to shape a chimney and snow
drifts around the cottage. Using royal icing, pipe icicles
at the roof edges and attach and decorate the shutters
and door.

Decorate with marshmallows and sweets. Lightly dust
the cottage and board with icing sugar.

christmas stocking

Serves **10**
Preparation time **1 hour**

1 roasting-tin **Madeira Cake**
(see page 10)
425 g (14 oz) **blue ready-to-roll icing**
¼ quantity **Royal Icing** (see page 10)
75 g (3 oz) **white ready-to-roll icing**
a few **edible silver balls**
white writing icing
125 g (4 oz) **pink ready-to-roll icing**
selection of **candy canes**

Vanilla butter icing
100 g (4 oz) **unsalted butter,** softened
250 g (8 oz) **icing sugar**
1 tablespoon **milk**
1 teaspoon **vanilla extract**

Beat the butter and sugar together, then add the milk and vanilla extract and mix the butter icing to a spreading consistency.

Cut the cake into a stocking shape about 11 cm (4½ inches) wide at the top of the leg. Cut 3 different-sized gifts from the trimmings. Split the cake horizontally and sandwich with butter icing. Spread butter icing very thinly over the top and sides of the cake and over the gifts. Transfer to a cake board or plate.

Reserve 50 g (2 oz) of the blue icing and knead the rest on a surface lightly dusted with icing sugar until slightly softened. Roll out and drape over the whole cake. Smooth in place and trim off the excess.

Spread the royal icing over the stocking top, then rough up the surface to resemble fleecy stocking lining.

Knead and roll out the white icing. Using biscuit cutters, cut out crescent moons and star shapes. Stick the shapes and silver balls on to the stocking with dots of writing icing.

Knead and roll out the pink and reserved blue icings and use to cover the gifts. Cut ribbons from the trimmings and stick on to the gifts with writing icing. Place at the stocking top. Add the candy canes to the cake board or plate, placing 1 cane at the stocking top.

For chocolate Christmas stocking, replace 65 g (2½ oz) of the flour in the Madeira cake mixture (see page 10) with cocoa powder. Dissolve 8 teaspoons cocoa powder in 2 tablespoons boiling water and use in the butter icing instead of the milk and vanilla extract.

pistachio nut stollen

Serves **15**
Preparation time **40 minutes**,
  plus rising
Cooking time **50–60 minutes**

625 g (1¼ lb) **strong plain
  flour**
25 g (1 oz) **fresh yeast**,
  crumbled
300 ml (½ pint) lukewarm
  milk
75 g (3 oz) **caster sugar**
1 **egg**
1 teaspoon **vanilla extract**
grated rind of ½ **lemon**
½ teaspoon **salt**
175 g (6 oz) **butter**
175 g (6 oz) **cut mixed peel**
125 g (4 oz) **pistachio nuts**
175 g (6 oz) **icing sugar**
1 tablespoon **maraschino
  liqueur**
125 g (4 oz) **marzipan**
65 g (2½ oz) melted **butter**,
  to glaze

Sift 500 g (1 lb) of the flour into a bowl, reserving a little sifted flour for sprinkling. Make a well, add the yeast and milk and stir into the flour. Sprinkle with a little flour, cover the bowl and leave for 20 minutes.

Add the sugar, egg, vanilla extract, lemon rind and salt to the yeast and knead to give a dry, firm dough. Cover the bowl and leave to rise for 10 minutes.

Work the butter together with the remaining flour and the mixed peel. Work this mixture into the dough and leave to rise for a further 30 minutes.

Work the pistachios, 50 g (2 oz) of the icing sugar and the maraschino into the marzipan. Roll out to 1 cm (½ inch) thick and cut into 1 cm (½ inch) cubes. Work these quickly into the dough. Shape the dough into 2 balls, then roll into 2 stollen about 30 cm (12 inches) long. Place on a baking sheet lined with greased greaseproof paper. Cover with greased clingfilm and leave to rise for 20–30 minutes.

Bake in a preheated oven, 200°C (400°F), Gas Mark 6, for 50–60 minutes, or until a skewer comes out clean. Brush the warm stollen all over with melted butter and dust with the remaining icing sugar.

For Austrian stollen, steep 140 g (4½ oz) raisins, 4 tablespoons blanched chopped almonds and 75 g (3 oz) cut mixed peel in 1 tablespoon rum. Use only 50 g (2 oz) caster sugar and raise the quantity of butter worked in to 250 g (8 oz). Omit the mixed peel, pistachios, icing sugar, maraschino and marzipan, and instead work the steeped fruit into the dough. Leave to rise for 30 minutes and continue as above.

american fruit & nut ring

Serves **12**

Preparation time **30 minutes**, plus cooling

Cooking time about **1¾ hours**

175 g (6 oz) **pitted ready-to-eat prunes**, finely chopped

125 g (4 oz) **dried apricot halves**, finely chopped

6 tablespoons **dark rum**

175 g (6 oz) **unsalted butter**, softened

175 g (6 oz) **soft dark brown sugar**

3 **eggs**

125 g (4 oz) **wholemeal flour**

125 g (4 oz) **plain flour**

¾ teaspoon **baking powder**

¾ teaspoon **ground allspice**

¼ teaspoon **ground ginger**

125 g (4 oz) **chopped nuts**

175 g (6 oz) **raisins**

grated rind of 1 **lemon**

grated rind of 1 **orange**

1 tablespoon **black treacle**

Topping

about 4 tablespoons **redcurrant jelly**, melted

mixed nuts

pitted ready-to-eat prunes

glacé cherries

Grease and line the sides of a 25 cm (10 inch) springform funnel tin with 2 strips of nonstick baking paper or greased greaseproof paper.

Soak the prunes and apricots in rum together for about 15 minutes while you are preparing the rest of the ingredients.

Cream the butter and sugar together until pale and very light and fluffy. Beat in the eggs, one at a time, following each with 1 tablespoon wholemeal flour. Sift the plain flour with the baking powder and spices and fold in with the remaining wholemeal flour. Mix in all the other ingredients including the soaked fruit plus any excess liquid in the bowl.

Turn into the tin, around the funnel, and level the top. Tie a piece of newspaper, folded into a treble thickness, around the outside of the tin. Bake in a preheated oven, 150°C (300°F), Gas Mark 2, for about 1¾ hours or until a skewer inserted in the cake comes out clean. Leave in the tin until cold, then remove carefully and peel off the lining paper.

Brush the cake with the redcurrant jelly, then arrange the nuts, prunes and cherries decoratively on the top. Brush again with more jelly and leave to set.

For cherry & nut ring, omit the dried apricots and use 125 g (4 oz) finely chopped glacé cherries instead. Steep the prunes and cherries in 6 tablespoons cherry brandy instead of rum.

smiling snowman

Serves **12**
Preparation time **1 hour**

2 pudding-basin **Madeira
  Cakes** (see page 10)
½ quantity **Vanilla Butter Icing**
  (see page 120)
2 tablespoons **smooth
  apricot jam**
1 large **ready-made muffin**
1½ quantities **Royal Icing** (see
  page 10)
25 g (1 oz) **orange ready-to-
  roll icing**
15 g (½ oz) **black ready-to-
  roll icing**
50 g (2 oz) **red ready-to-roll
  icing**
25 g (1 oz) **yellow ready-to-
  roll icing**
icing sugar, for dusting

Sandwich the cakes with the butter icing to make the snowman's body and stand upright on a cake board or plate. Spread jam thinly all over the outside of the cakes to stick the crumbs in place. Press the muffin on to the body so that its domed part forms the snowman's face. Spread the muffin with the remaining jam.

Cover the cakes completely with royal icing, spreading with a round-bladed knife and pulling it into peaks with the back of the knife.

Knead the ready-to-roll icing on a surface lightly dusted with icing sugar until slightly softened, keeping the colours separate. Shape an orange carrot nose and black pebble eyes, a black mouth and black buttons. Press on to the snowman. Shape half the red icing into a round and press on to the snowman's head for a hat. Use a strip of yellow icing as a hatband.

Shape the rest of the yellow icing into a rope 18 cm (7 inches) long. Repeat with the remaining orange and red icing. Twist together, roll out to flatten and trim to a 36 x 2.5 cm (14 x 1 inch) scarf. Make small cuts in either end for a fringe, then wrap around the snowman. Re-knead and roll out the trimmings, fringe one side, then roll up and add to the top of the hat for a bobble. Dust with sifted icing sugar for freshly fallen snow.

For lemony snowman, omit the royal icing and instead make up 1 quantity of Vanilla Butter Icing (see page 120), omitting the milk and adding 2 teaspoons grated lemon rind and 1 tablespoon lemon juice to the mixture. Use to sandwich the cakes and to cover the snowman. Otherwise, prepare as above.

panforte di siena

Serves **15**
Preparation time **20 minutes**,
  plus cooling
Cooking time **55 minutes**

75 g (3 oz) **hazelnuts**,
  toasted, skinned and
  chopped
75 g (3 oz) **blanched**
  almonds, toasted and
  chopped
75 g (3 oz) **candied orange**
  peel, chopped
75 g (3 oz) **candied lemon**
  peel, chopped
75 g (3 oz) **candied fruit**,
  chopped
2 teaspoons **ground**
  cinnamon
large pinch of **ground mixed**
  spice
75 g (3 oz) **plain flour**
125 g (4 oz) **thick honey**
100 g (3½ oz) **caster sugar**
icing sugar, for dusting

Line a deep sponge cake tin or a loose-bottomed 18–20 cm (7–8 inch) round cake tin with rice paper. Combine the nuts, peel and fruit, then sift in the spices and flour and stir until evenly mixed.

Put the honey and caster sugar into a saucepan and bring slowly to the boil. Pour over the nut mixture and stir well until blended and a sticky mass forms.

Place the mixture in the tin, but don't press down too firmly. Bake in a preheated oven, 150°C (300°F), Gas Mark 2, for about 50 minutes or until almost firm to the touch.

Cool in the tin and then remove carefully. If the rice paper is torn or pulled away from the cake, add a new layer, attaching it with a dab of lightly beaten egg white. Dust the top heavily with icing sugar and serve cut into thin wedges.

For chocolate & date panforte, replace 1 tablespoon of the flour with good-quality cocoa powder and replace half the candied orange and lemon peel with 75 g (3 oz) chopped dates. After dusting the top heavily with icing sugar, sift extra cocoa powder over a simple stencil to make an attractive pattern on top.

tropical christmas cake

Serves **10**
Preparation time **30 minutes**,
  plus cooling
Cooking time **1¼–1½ hours**

300 g (10 oz) **unsalted butter**
200 g (7 oz) **caster sugar**
3 large **eggs**, beaten
425 g (14 oz) **self-raising
  flour**
250 g (8 oz) **pineapple rings
  in syrup**
75 g (3 oz) **glacé cherries**,
  chopped
50 g (2 oz) **cut mixed peel**
3 tablespoons chopped
  angelica
3 tablespoons chopped
  walnuts
3 tablespoons **desiccated
  coconut**
75 g (3 oz) **sultanas**
2 tablespoons toasted
  coconut shavings, to
  decorate

Coconut icing
45 g (1½ oz) **unsalted butter**
250 g (8 oz) **icing sugar**
2 tablespoons **desiccated
  coconut**

Grease a 23 cm (9 inch) ring mould or 20 cm (8 inch) cake tin and line with nonstick baking paper or greased greaseproof paper. Cream the butter and sugar until soft and light, then gradually beat in the eggs. Sift the flour and fold into the creamed mixture.

Drain the canned pineapple, setting aside 1 tablespoon of the syrup for the icing and 3 tablespoons of the syrup for the cake. Chop the pineapple rings finely. Fold the dried fruit, nuts and pineapple into the cake mixture with the coconut, sultanas and the 3 tablespoons of pineapple syrup.

Put the mixture into the ring mould or cake tin. Bake in a preheated oven, 160°C (325°F), Gas Mark 3, for 1¼ hours if using a ring mould and 1½ hours if using a cake tin. Cool for at least 10 minutes in the tin, then turn out on to a wire rack and leave to cool completely.

Melt the butter for the icing in a pan, then remove from the heat. Sift in the icing sugar, then add the remaining pineapple syrup and the coconut. Stir to combine, then spread the icing over the top of the cake and a little down the sides. Sprinkle with toasted coconut shavings.

For ginger cake, omit the pineapple, cherries, mixed peel, angelica, walnuts, coconut and sultanas and instead chop 5 pieces of stem ginger in syrup and stir into the cake mixture with 2 tablespoons of the syrup, 1 teaspoon ground ginger, 1 teaspoon grated fresh root ginger and 2 tablespoons milk. For the icing, replace the pineapple syrup and coconut with 2 pieces of chopped stem ginger and the juice of 1 lemon.

small cakes
& cookies

rich mince pies

Makes **12**
Preparation time **20 minutes**
Cooking time **20 minutes**

250 g (8 oz) **plain flour**
75 g (3 oz) chilled **unsalted butter**, diced
50 g (2 oz) **ground almonds**
25 g (1 oz) **caster sugar**, plus extra for sprinkling
grated rind of 1 **orange**
1 **egg**, beaten
2–3 tablespoons **orange juice**
250 g (8 oz) **mincemeat**
a little **milk** or beaten **egg**, to glaze

Place the flour in a bowl, add the butter and rub in with the fingertips until the mixture resembles fine breadcrumbs. Stir in the ground almonds, sugar and orange rind, then add the beaten egg and orange juice and mix to a firm dough.

Knead the dough briefly on a lightly floured surface, then roll out thinly and stamp out 12 x 8 cm (3½ inch) rounds with a pastry cutter. Line 12 bun tins with the pastry, pressing the pastry rounds into the tins. Add 1 teaspoon mincemeat to each case.

Roll out the remaining pastry and cut into 5 cm (2 inch) rounds to cover the mince pies. Use a small star cutter to cut out stars from half the pastry lids.

Dampen the edges of the cases and press the lids down lightly to seal them. Brush the tops of the pies with a little milk or beaten egg and sprinkle lightly with the sugar.

Bake in a preheated oven, 200°C (400°F), Gas Mark 6, for 20 minutes until golden. Leave to cool slightly in the tins, then transfer to a wire rack to cool completely.

For puff pastry mince pies, thinly roll out 500 g (1 lb) ready-made puff pastry. Cut into rounds and fill with mincemeat as above. Brush each pie with a little beaten egg or milk and sprinkle with flaked almonds. Bake at the above temperature for 20–25 minutes or until puffed and golden.

christmas stars

Makes **12**

Preparation time **35 minutes**, plus cooling

Cooking time **18–20 minutes**

50 g (2 oz) **white ready-to-roll icing**

Orange Butter Icing (see page 140)

25 g (1 oz) **desiccated coconut**

Fairy cakes

150 g (5 oz) **unsalted butter**, softened

150 g (5 oz) **caster sugar**

175 g (6 oz) **self-raising flour**

3 **eggs**

1 teaspoon **vanilla extract**

Line a 12-section bun tray with paper cake cases. Beat all the cake ingredients together until light and creamy. Divide the mixture evenly among the cake cases. Bake in a preheated oven, 180°C (350°F), Gas Mark 4, for 18–20 minutes until risen and just firm to the touch. Transfer to a wire rack to cool.

Knead the white ready-to-roll icing on a surface lightly dusted with icing sugar until slightly softened. Roll out thickly and cut out star shapes using a small star-shaped biscuit cutter. Transfer to a baking sheet lined with nonstick baking paper and leave to harden while decorating the cakes.

Spread the icing roughly over the cakes and scatter with coconut. Gently press 2 stars into the top of each cake and leave to set.

For chocolate Christmas stars, make the fairy cakes as above, substituting 15 g (½ oz) cocoa powder for 15 g (½ oz) of the flour. Replace the orange butter icing with chocolate butter icing, made by beating together 75 g (3 oz) softened unsalted butter, 125 g (4 oz) icing sugar and 1 tablespoon cocoa powder dissolved in 1 tablespoon boiling water until smooth. Bake and decorate as above.

mini iced gingerbread cakes

Makes **12**
Preparation time **10 minutes**,
  plus cooling
Cooking time **15–20 minutes**

125 g (4 oz) **unsalted butter**
250 g (8 oz) **golden syrup**
75 g (3 oz) **dark muscovado
  sugar**
250 g (8 oz) **self-raising flour**
1 teaspoon **ground ginger**
1 teaspoon **ground mixed
  spice**
½ teaspoon **bicarbonate of
  soda**
150 ml (¼ pint) **milk**
2 **eggs**
125 g (4 oz) **icing sugar**
4 teaspoons **water**
glacé cherries, chopped

Line a 12-section muffin tin with large muffin cases.
Put the butter, syrup and sugar in a saucepan. Heat
gently, stirring with a wooden spoon, until the butter
has completely melted.

Take the pan off the heat. Sift the flour, spices and
bicarbonate of soda into a bowl. Beat the milk and
eggs together in a jug with a fork. Add the dry
ingredients to the pan, mix with a wooden spoon, then
gradually beat in the milk mixture until smooth.

Pour the gingerbread mixture into the muffin cases
until two-thirds full. Bake in the centre of a preheated
oven, 180°C (350°F), Gas Mark 4, for 10–15 minutes
until well risen and the tops spring back when pressed
with the fingertips. Cool in the tin.

Sift the icing sugar into a bowl. Gradually mix in the
measured water to make a smooth, thick icing. Scatter
the cherries over the cakes, drizzle with the icing and
leave to set.

For snow-covered ginger muffins, stir 3 tablespoons
chopped candied ginger into the mix before pouring
into the cases, then bake as above. To decorate, mix
4 teaspoons water with 200 g (7 oz) sifted icing sugar
to make a smooth, spoonable icing. Drizzle lines of
icing over the cakes and top with small slices of
candied ginger. Allow to set before serving.

christmas trees

Serves **12**
Preparation time **25 minutes**

1 roasting-tin **Madeira Cake**
  (see page 10)
green and **silver sugar pearls**
12 **white marshmallows**

Orange butter icing
125 g (4 oz) **unsalted butter**,
  softened
250 g (8 oz) **icing sugar**,
  sifted
grated rind of 1 **orange** and
  1 tablespoon of the juice

Place the butter in a bowl and gradually beat in the icing sugar until light and fluffy. Stir in the orange rind and juice.

Cut the cake horizontally into 3 short strips. Cut each strip into 3 triangles and use the half-triangle left at each end to make a fourth triangle, butting the halves together with a little butter icing. Create a total of 12 triangles – 9 whole ones and 3 made of butted-together halves.

Spread the tops and sides of the cakes thinly with butter icing to stick the crumbs in place, then spread with a thicker layer of icing. Arrange the triangles on a cake board or plate.

Place a marshmallow at the base of each triangle for a tub. Press on sugar pearls for decorations.

For chocolate Christmas trees, follow the recipe for the Madeira cake (see page 10), substituting 40 g (1½ oz) cocoa powder for the same weight of flour and increasing the quantity of baking powder to 1½ teaspoons. Use large chocolates for the tubs. Alternatively, cut a small strip of sponge off the cake before making the triangles, cut the strip into 12 for the tubs and wrap each one in red ready-to-roll icing.

mini christmas cakes

Makes **12**

Preparation time **30 minutes**, plus cooling

Cooking time **25 minutes**

150 g (5 oz) **unsalted butter**
150 g (5 oz) **light muscovado sugar**
200 g (7 oz) **self-raising flour**
3 **eggs**
1 teaspoon **almond extract**
50 g (2 oz) **chopped nuts**
75 g (3 oz) **mixed dried fruit**
2 tablespoons **smooth apricot jam**
175 g (6 oz) **icing sugar**
4–5 teaspoons cold **water**
25 g (1 oz) **green ready-to-roll icing**
25 g (1 oz) **red ready-to-roll icing**

Marzipan
100 g (3½ oz) **ground hazelnuts** or **almonds**
50 g (2 oz) **caster sugar**
50 g (2 oz) **icing sugar**
a few drops of **yellow food colouring**
1 tablespoon **egg white**

Line a 12-section bun tray with paper cake cases. Put the butter, sugar, flour, eggs and almond extract in a mixing bowl and beat for 1–2 minutes until light and creamy. Add the nuts and dried fruit and stir in until evenly combined. Divide the mixture evenly among the cake cases. Bake in a preheated oven, 180°C (350°F), Gas Mark 4, for 25 minutes until risen and just firm to the touch. Transfer to a wire rack to cool.

Put the nuts, sugars and food colouring for the marzipan in a bowl. Add the egg white and mix with a round-bladed knife until the mixture starts to cling together. Finish mixing the paste by hand until smooth and very firm. Lightly knead and shape into a thick sausage, 8 cm (3½ inches) long. Cut into 12 slices.

Spread ½ teaspoon jam on the centre of each cake, then place a marzipan slice on top.

Put the icing sugar in a bowl and add the measured water to make a thick smooth paste – the icing should hold its shape but not feel too firm. Gently spread the icing over the marzipan.

Knead and roll out the green and red ready-to-roll icing and use to make small holly leaves and berries. Press on to the tops of the cakes to decorate.

For snow-dusted Christmas cakes, make the fairy cakes as above. Thinly spread smooth apricot jam over the tops, then dust liberally with sifted icing sugar. Top with edible holly leaf decorations made of marzipan or royal icing (see page 10).

reindeer cupcakes

Makes **12**

Preparation time **40 minutes**,
plus cooling

Cooking time **13–15 minutes**

1 tablespoon **cocoa powder**
1 tablespoon boiling **water**
125 g (4 oz) **unsalted butter**,
softened
2 **eggs**
125 g (4 oz) **caster sugar**
125 g (4 oz) **self-raising flour**
150 g (5 oz) **plain dark
chocolate**, broken into
pieces
6 **glacé cherries**, halved
1 small packet **candy-coated
chocolate drops**

Icing
1 tablespoon **cocoa powder**
1 tablespoon boiling **water**
50 g (2 oz) **unsalted butter**,
softened
125 g (4 oz) **icing sugar**

Line a 12-section bun tray with red foil cake cases.
Put the cocoa powder into a bowl and mix to a smooth
paste with the boiling water.

Put the butter, eggs, caster sugar and flour into a bowl
and beat until smooth. Stir in the cocoa paste, then
divide the mixture among the paper cake cases. Bake
in a preheated oven, 180°C (350°F), Gas Mark 4, for
13–15 minutes until they are well risen and spring
back when pressed with a fingertip. Leave to cool.

Melt the chocolate in a heatproof bowl over a pan of
gently simmering water. Spoon most of the melted
chocolate (reserve a little and keep warm in the bowl)
into a paper piping bag, snip off the tip and pipe lines
of chocolate about 6 cm (2½ inches) long on a baking
tray lined with nonstick baking paper. Pipe on branches
for antlers. Make enough for 2 per cake, with extras in
case of breakages.

Mix the icing cocoa powder with the boiling water. Add
the butter, then gradually beat in the icing sugar until
smooth. Spread over the tops of the cupcakes.

Add to each a cherry half for a nose and 2 chocolate
drops for eyes, piping on the remaining melted
chocolate to make eyeballs. Peel the set antlers off the
baking paper and stick at angles into the cupcakes.

For Christmas robin cakes, make the cakes as
above and spread the chocolate icing smoothly over
the tops. Use melted chocolate to pipe the outline
of a robin on each cake. Finish by adding a sliver of
glacé cherry for the robin's red breast.

baby panettones

Makes **8**

Preparation time **25 minutes**,
plus rising

Cooking time **20–25 minutes**

2 teaspoons **easy-blend
dried yeast**

125 g (4 oz) **caster sugar**,
plus 1 teaspoon

175 ml (6 fl oz) hand-hot **milk**

700 g (1 lb 6 oz) **strong
bread flour**

4 large **eggs**, plus 2 **yolks**

2 teaspoons **vanilla extract**

finely grated rind of
2 **lemons**

175 g (6 oz) **salted butter**,
very soft and diced

175 g (6 oz) **mixed dried fruit**

Grease 8 x 400 ml (14 fl oz) clean food cans and line with greaseproof paper that extends above the rims. Grease the paper. Stir the yeast and 1 teaspoon sugar into the milk in a large, warm bowl and leave for 10 minutes or until frothy. Stir in 100 g (3½ oz) of the flour. Cover with clingfilm and leave for 30 minutes.

Add the eggs and yolks, the remaining flour and the sugar, vanilla extract, lemon rind and butter. Mix with a round-bladed knife to make a soft dough, adding a little more flour if the dough feels sticky. Turn out on to a lightly floured surface and knead until smooth and elastic. Leave to rise in a lightly greased bowl, covered with clingfilm, for 2–4 hours or until doubled in size.

Knock back the dough (punch your fist into the risen dough so that it collapses as the air is excluded) and lightly knead in the dried fruit. Cut the dough into 8 pieces and drop into the tins. Cover and leave to rise until the dough almost reaches the rims.

Bake in a preheated oven, 200°C (400°F), Gas Mark 6, for 20–25 minutes or until risen and golden. Leave for 5 minutes, then cool on a wire rack.

For whole panettone, shape the mixture into 1 large ball. Place in a 15 cm (6 inch) round cake tin, greased and lined with a double layer of greased greaseproof paper that extends 10 cm (4 inches) above the rim. Cover and leave to rise. Bake for 15 minutes at 200°C (400°F), Gas Mark 6, then reduce to 180°C (350°F), Gas Mark 4, and bake for 40 minutes until well risen and an inserted skewer comes out clean. Leave for 10 minutes, then cool on a wire rack.

marzipan & apple pies

Makes **12**
Preparation time **10–15 minutes**, plus chilling
Cooking time **15–20 minutes**

125 g (4 oz) **plain flour**
125 g (4 oz) **wholemeal flour**
pinch of **salt**
125 g (4 oz) **unsalted butter**, chilled
3–4 tablespoons **water**
200 g (7 oz) **cooking apples**, peeled, cored and coarsely chopped
75 g (3 oz) **marzipan**, cut into 5 mm (¼ inch) cubes
milk, for brushing
1 tablespoon **demerara sugar** (optional)

Mix the flours and salt in a bowl, then grate in the butter. Distribute the butter gently through the flour, using a round-bladed knife, then add the measured water and mix to a fairly firm dough. Put the pastry into a polythene bag and chill in the refrigerator for 1 hour, if possible.

Roll out the pastry thinly on a lightly floured surface. Cut out 12 rounds using a 8 cm (3½ inch) fluted cutter and 12 rounds using a 5 cm (2 inch) fluted cutter. Line a 12-section bun tray with the larger rounds.

Mix the apples and marzipan together in a bowl. Spoon the mixture into the pastry cases, packing it in well.

Brush both sides of the remaining rounds with milk and lay them on top of the tartlets in the tin. Press the edges together to seal and sprinkle each one with a little demerara sugar, if liked. Bake near the top of a preheated oven, 220°C (425°F), Gas Mark 7, for 15–20 minutes until golden brown. Remove carefully from the tins and leave to cool slightly on a wire rack. Serve warm or cold.

For pear & marzipan pastries, replace the apples with 200 g (7 oz) pears, peeled, cored and coarsely chopped. Combine with the marzipan. Thinly roll out 375 g (12 oz) ready-made puff pastry and cut into 6 x 10 cm (4 inch) squares. Top each one with a spoonful of pear and marzipan filling and fold in half to form triangular parcels. Seal the edges and prick holes in the top. Brush with milk, dredge with caster sugar and bake as above for 20 minutes until risen and golden.

meringue snowmen

Makes **9–12**
Preparation time **20 minutes**
Cooking time **45–60 minutes**

3 **egg whites**
125 g (4 oz) **caster sugar**
currants
glacé cherries, cut into pieces
cut mixed peel (optional)

Line a baking sheet with nonstick baking paper. Whisk the egg whites in a large bowl until they form soft peaks. Whisk in the sugar, a teaspoon at a time, until it has all been added and you have a thick, glossy meringue mixture. You should be able to hold the bowl upside down without the mixture falling out.

Use a teaspoon to place a meringue head on a baking sheet, then use a tablespoon for the snowman's body. Repeat to make 9–12 snowmen. Attach currants for their eyes and pieces of glacé cherry for their mouths. Give them buttons down their fronts using more currants or pieces of mixed peel.

Bake in a preheated oven, 110°C (225°F), Gas Mark ¼, for 45–60 minutes or until the meringues are firm and may be easily peeled off the paper. Allow to cool on the baking sheet.

For marron meringues, make the meringue mix as above and place in a piping bag fitted with a large star nozzle. Pipe 10 cm (4 inch) bars on the lined baking sheet and cook as above. To assemble, beat 265 g (8½ oz) sweetened chestnut purée with 1 tablespoon rum or coffee liqueur until smooth. Whip 150 ml (¼ pint) double cream until stiff and fold through the chestnut mixture. Use the chestnut cream to sandwich the meringues in pairs. Makes 8–10 meringues.

tree decorations

Makes **25**
Preparation time **40 minutes**,
  plus cooling
Cooking time **15–17 minutes**

75 g (3 oz) **unsalted butter**
4 tablespoons **golden syrup**
100 g (3½ oz) **caster sugar**
1 teaspoon **ground cinnamon**
½ teaspoon **ground ginger**
large pinch of **ground allspice**
300 g (10 oz) **plain flour**
1 teaspoon **bicarbonate of
  soda**
about 3 tablespoons **milk**
125 g (4 oz) **white writing
  icing**
a few **edible coloured balls**
  (optional)

Put the butter, syrup and sugar into a saucepan and heat gently, stirring occasionally, until the butter has melted and the sugar dissolved. Take the pan off the heat and stir in the spices. Mix together the flour and bicarbonate of soda and then beat into the spicy butter mixture, adding enough milk to make a smooth dough.

Turn out the dough on to a board and leave it for 5–10 minutes until it is cool enough to handle. Knead well, then roll out on a lightly floured surface or a piece of nonstick baking paper.

Cut out Christmas shapes using star, tree, stocking, bell or any other festive cutters. Re-roll the trimmings and cut out more shapes. Transfer the shapes to lightly greased baking sheets.

Make a hole in the top of each biscuit with the end of a skewer or a teaspoon handle and bake in a preheated oven, 180°C (350°F), Gas Mark 4, for 10–12 minutes until browned. Enlarge the hole for ribbon if needed. Allow to cool on the baking sheets.

Pipe the icing on to the biscuits, add the coloured balls, if using, and allow to harden. Thread fine ribbons through the holes on the biscuits and tie on to the Christmas tree.

For children's tree cookies, make the biscuit dough, cut out tree shapes (omitting the holes) and bake as above. When cool, decorate the tree biscuits using different coloured writing icing to represent tinsel and mini candy-coated chocolate drops as baubles.

chocolate viennese whirls

Makes **12**
Preparation time **15 minutes**,
  plus cooling
Cooking time **15–20 minutes**

200 g (7 oz) **unsalted butter**,
  softened
100 g (3½ oz) **caster sugar**
200 g (7 oz) **plain flour**
½ teaspoon **baking powder**
25 g (1 oz) **cocoa powder**
2 teaspoons **milk**
100 g (3½ oz) **plain dark
  chocolate**, broken into
  pieces

Line a 12-section bun tray with paper cake cases. Beat together the butter and sugar until pale and creamy. Sift the flour, baking powder and cocoa powder into the bowl, add the milk and beat well to make a smooth paste.

Spoon the mixture into a piping bag fitted with a large star nozzle and pipe rings into the paper cases, leaving a large hole in the centre.

Bake the whirls in a preheated oven, 190°C (375°F), Gas Mark 5, for 15–20 minutes or until slightly risen. Press a hole in the centre of each one. Allow to cool in the tin.

Melt the chocolate in a heatproof bowl over a pan of gently simmering water. Spoon a little chocolate into the centre of each Viennese whirl. Allow to set slightly before serving.

For raspberry Viennese whirls, make the Viennese mixture as above, using 100 g (3½ oz) icing sugar instead of the caster sugar and replacing the cocoa powder and milk with 1 teaspoon vanilla essence. Pipe the mixture into cake cases as above, then press a still-frozen raspberry into the centre of each cake before baking. Leave to cool in the tin, then add tiny spoonfuls of seedless raspberry jam instead of the melted chocolate to the centre of each cake. Dust lightly with icing sugar and serve.

3D winter wonderland

Makes **1 winter scene**
Preparation time **about
1½ hours**, plus cooling
and setting
Cooking time **15 minutes**

double quantity **Spicy
Gingerbread dough**, chilled
(see page 158)
½ quantity **Royal Icing** (see
page 10)
125 g (4 oz) **red ready-to-roll
icing**
25 g (1 oz) **black ready-to-
roll icing**
icing sugar, for dusting

Roll out the gingerbread dough on a lightly floured
surface and cut out shapes using a set of Christmas
scene cutters. You'll need 2 sleigh sides, 2 sleigh ends,
2 reindeer bodies and 4 pairs of legs, 1 snowman with
base and 1 tree with base. Place the pieces on large
greased baking sheets, spacing them slightly apart.

Bake in a preheated oven, 180°C (350°F), Gas Mark
4, for 15 minutes or until the dough has risen slightly
and is darkening at the edges. Leave for 5 minutes,
then transfer to wire racks to cool.

Put the royal icing in a pastry bag fitted with a plain
nozzle. Knead the red ready-to-roll icing until slightly
softened, roll out thinly and cut out 4 top sections
for the sleigh sides using the same cutter as before.
Attach using piped royal icing. Roll out the black icing
and cut out small squares for the reindeers' hooves.
Shape and secure small red reindeer noses and a red
scarf and black hat for the snowman.

Pipe royal icing decorations on the sleigh, reindeer,
snowman and tree. Leave to set for at least 1 hour.

Assemble the scene by slotting the pieces together.
Place on a board and dust lightly with icing sugar.

For gingerbread snowmen, use a snowman cutter to
cut out about 20 snowmen from a single quantity of
Spicy Gingerbread dough and bake as above. Lightly
knead 250 g (8 oz) white ready-to-roll icing, roll out
and cut 20 more snowmen. Stick the icing snowmen
on the cooled biscuits using piped royal icing. Add
a scarf and hat for each snowman as above and add
smiling faces using writing icing.

stencilled cookies

Makes **10**
Preparation time **25 minutes**,
 plus chilling and cooling
Cooking time **12 minutes**

Spicy gingerbread
125 g (4 oz) **unsalted butter**,
 softened
75 g (3 oz) **light brown sugar**
1 **egg**, beaten
5 tablespoons **black treacle**
375 g (12 oz) **self-raising
 flour**
1½ teaspoons **ground ginger**

Buttercream
50 g (2 oz) **unsalted butter**,
 softened
125 g (4 oz) **icing sugar**, plus
 extra for dusting
1 tablespoon **milk** or **cream**

Make the spicy gingerbread by beating the butter and sugar together until creamy. Stir in the egg and black treacle. Sift in the flour and ground ginger and stir to form a stiff paste. Turn out the dough on to a lightly floured work surface and knead lightly until smooth. Wrap and chill for at least 30 minutes before using.

Roll out the dough thinly on a lightly floured surface and cut out rounds using a 6 cm (2½ inch) round biscuit cutter. Place on greased baking sheets, spaced apart, and re-roll the trimmings to make extras. Bake in a preheated oven, 180°C (350°F), Gas Mark 4, for 12 minutes or until the dough has risen slightly and is darkening at the edges. Transfer to a wire rack to cool.

Beat together the butter and a little of the sugar. Gradually beat in the remaining sugar and the milk or cream until smooth. Use to sandwich the cookies together in pairs.

Make templates of a simple Christmas tree and star from 7 cm (3 inch) circles of paper. Lay a template over a cookie and dust with plenty of icing sugar. Carefully lift off the template, shake off excess sugar and repeat the decoration on the other cookies.

For spicy gingerbread people, make, chill and roll out the dough as above. Cut out shapes using gingerbread people cutters. Bake on greased baking sheets in a preheated oven, 180°C (350°F), Gas Mark 4, for 15 minutes or until the dough has risen slightly and is darkening at the edges. Cool on a wire rack, then decorate using writing icing, ready-to-roll icing, candy-coated chocolate drops and other sweets.

mulled wine biscuits

Makes about **25**
Preparation time **15 minutes**,
 plus cooling
Cooking time **25–30 minutes**

140 g (4½ oz) **raisins**
75 g (3 oz) **dried cranberries**
150 ml (¼ pint) **red wine**
100 g (3½ oz) **redcurrant jelly**
pinch of **chilli powder**
1 teaspoon **ground cinnamon**
¼ teaspoon **ground cloves**
50 g (2 oz) **walnuts**, chopped
50 g (2 oz) **blanched
 almonds**, chopped
100 g (3½ oz) **plain dark
 chocolate**, finely chopped
75 g (3 oz) **self-raising flour**
finely grated rind of **1 orange**
50 g (2 oz) **unsalted butter**,
 melted
1 egg
icing sugar, for dusting

Put the raisins and cranberries in a small heavy-based saucepan with the wine, redcurrant jelly and spices. Heat until the jelly dissolves, then bring to the boil and boil for 2–3 minutes until the syrup is reduced by about half. Allow to cool.

Mix the nuts and chocolate in a bowl with the flour, orange rind, butter, egg and fruit mixture to make a paste. Place teaspoons of the mixture, spaced slightly apart, on a lightly greased baking sheet.

Bake the biscuits in a preheated oven, 180°C (350°F), Gas Mark 4, for about 20 minutes until they have spread slightly. Leave them on the baking sheet for 3 minutes, then transfer to a wire rack to cool. Dust generously with icing sugar.

For port & cherry cookies, omit the dried cranberries and the red wine and use 75 g (3 oz) dried cherries and 150 ml (¼ pint) inexpensive port instead. Replace the blanched almonds with 50 g (2 oz) chopped hazelnuts and continue as above.

triple chocolate biscotti

Makes **about 28**
Preparation time **35 minutes**,
  plus cooling
Cooking time **45 minutes**

50 g (2 oz) **lightly salted
  butter**, softened
50 g (2 oz) **caster sugar**
175 g (6 oz) **self-raising flour**
1 teaspoon **baking powder**
½ teaspoon **ground coriander**
finely grated rind of **1 orange**,
  plus **1 tablespoon** of the juice
50 g (2 oz) **polenta**
1 **egg**, lightly beaten
100 g (3½ oz) **unblanched
  almonds**, roughly chopped
75 g (3 oz) **milk chocolate
  chips**
150 g (5 oz) **plain dark
  chocolate**, broken into
  pieces
50 g (2 oz) **white chocolate**,
  broken into pieces

Beat the butter and sugar until creamy. Add the flour, baking powder, coriander, orange rind and juice, polenta and egg and mix to form a firm dough. Knead in the almonds. Turn out the dough on a lightly floured surface and gently work in the chocolate chips. Divide the mixture in half and shape each piece into a log about 23 cm (9 inches) long.

Place on a greased baking sheet, spaced well apart, and flatten slightly. Bake in a preheated oven, 160°C (325°F), Gas Mark 3, for 30 minutes or until risen and just firm. Remove from the oven and cool on the baking sheet for 15 minutes. Transfer to a board and, using a serrated knife, cut into 1 cm (½ inch) thick slices.

Arrange on the baking sheet, cut sides down, and bake for 15 minutes until crisp. Transfer to a wire rack and leave to cool.

Melt the plain dark and white chocolate in 2 separate heatproof bowls over pans of simmering water. Line a tray or clean baking sheet with nonstick baking paper. Dip about one-third of each biscuit in the plain dark chocolate, letting the excess fall back into the bowl. Place each biscuit on the baking paper.

Drizzle thin lines of melted white chocolate over the plain dark chocolate to decorate. Leave in a cool place to set for about 1 hour.

For chocolate & walnut biscotti, omit the ground coriander and almonds and instead use 1 teaspoon vanilla essence and 125 g (4 oz) chopped walnut pieces. Replace the milk chocolate chips with white chocolate chips and continue as above.

candy cane cookies

Makes **28–30**
Preparation time **50 minutes**,
  plus cooling
Cooking time **15 minutes**

1 quantity **Vanilla Biscuits
  dough**, chilled (see page
  168)
½ quantity **Royal Icing** (see
  page 10)

First make the candy cane template. On paper draw a
walking stick, 1 cm (½ inch) wide and 10 cm (4 inches)
long, with a curved end, then cut it out. Roll out the
biscuit dough on a lightly floured surface. Lay the
template over the dough and cut around it about 25
times using a small, sharp knife or scalpel.

Space the shapes slightly apart on greased baking
sheets. Re-roll the trimmings to make extras. Bake
in a preheated oven, 180°C (350°F), Gas Mark 4,
for 15 minutes or until pale golden. Transfer to a wire
rack to cool.

Put the royal icing in a pastry bag fitted with a plain
nozzle and pipe a zig-zag line of icing along each
cookie. Leave the cookies in a cool place to set for at
least 1 hour before serving.

For Christmas baubles, cut the dough into 20 x
7.5 cm (3¼ inch) rounds. Use a skewer to make a
small hole 1 cm (½ inch) in from the edge of each
circle. Bake as above, re-piercing the holes as soon
as the biscuits come out of the oven. When cool,
brush the cookies with smooth apricot jam and
sprinkle over bands of green and red sugar sprinkles.
Pipe royal icing between the sugar sprinkles and
around the edges. Leave to set for at least 1 hour
before threading with thin ribbon.

hazelnut meringues

Makes **25**
Preparation time **20 minutes**
Cooking time **45–60 minutes**

100 g (3½ oz) **hazelnuts**
4 **egg whites**
225 g (7½ oz) **caster sugar**
½ teaspoon **white wine vinegar**
¼ teaspoon **vanilla extract**
100 g (3½ oz) **crème fraîche**
175 g (6 oz) **redcurrants**

Line a baking sheet with nonstick baking paper. Coarsely grind the hazelnuts in a food processor (or chop them and then crush with a pestle and mortar), then set them aside.

Whisk the egg whites in a large bowl until they form soft peaks. Gradually add the sugar, a teaspoon at a time, whisking until the mixture is very stiff and shiny. The mixture should stay put, even when the bowl is tilted. Fold in the vinegar and vanilla extract, then fold in the ground nuts.

Spoon the meringue mixture on to the lined baking sheet, to make approximately 25 mini meringues, spacing them apart as they will expand slightly in the oven. Bake in a preheated oven, 110°C (225°F), Gas Mark ¼, for 45–60 minutes or until the meringues are firm and may be easily peeled off the paper.

Allow to cool on the baking sheet. Serve the cooled meringues topped with a little crème fraîche and a small sprig of redcurrants.

For rosewater, cinnamon & orange meringues, replace the hazelnuts with the finely grated rind of 1 orange and replace the vanilla extract with 3 drops rosewater and a large pinch of ground cinnamon. Fold in with the vinegar, as above.

falling snowflakes

Makes **14**

Preparation time **50 minutes**,
  plus chilling and cooling

Cooking time **15 minutes**

½ quantity **Royal Icing** (see
  page 10)

Vanilla biscuits
250 g (8 oz) **plain flour**
250 g (8 oz) chilled **unsalted
  butter**, diced
125 g (4 oz) **icing sugar**
2 **egg yolks**
2 teaspoons **vanilla extract**

Citrus glaze
8 teaspoons **lemon**, **lime** or
  orange juice
250 g (8 oz) **icing sugar**

Combine the flour and butter until the mix resembles
fine breadcrumbs. Add the sugar, egg yolks and vanilla
extract and whiz to a smooth dough. Wrap and chill for
at least 30 minutes before using.

Roll out the dough on a lightly floured surface and
cut out star shapes, using a 10 cm (4 inch) star biscuit
cutter. Space them slightly apart on greased baking
sheets, then re-roll the trimmings to make extras. Using
a skewer make a small hole on each star, near the tip
of a point. Bake in a preheated oven, 180°C (350°F),
Gas Mark 4, for 15 minutes or until pale golden.
Remove from the oven and immediately remake the
holes. Transfer to a wire rack to cool.

Place the citrus juice in a small bowl and gradually
beat in the sugar until the glaze thickly coats the back
of the spoon. Spread it over the biscuits almost to the
edges of each star.

Put the royal icing in a piping bag fitted with a plain
nozzle. Pipe 3 lines across each biscuit, then pipe a row
of tiny chevrons over each line to create a snowflake
effect. Leave in a cool place to set for at least 1 hour
before threading with thin ribbon.

For iced snowflakes, make and cook the biscuits as
above but omit the hole-making step. Omit the citrus
glaze. Lightly knead and roll out 250 g (8 oz) white
ready-to-roll icing. Use the biscuit cutter to make star
shapes from the icing and stick to the biscuits using a
little royal icing. Pipe the lines and chevrons on top of
the snowflakes as above.

gingerbread nightlights

Makes **4**

Preparation time **50 minutes**, plus cooling

Cooking time **13–15 minutes**

1 quantity **Spicy Gingerbread dough**, chilled (see page 158)

175 g (6 oz) **coloured boiled sweets**, lightly crushed

½ quantity **Royal Icing** (see page 10)

Roll out half the gingerbread dough thinly on a lightly floured surface and cut out a neat 36 x 18 cm (14 x 7 inch) rectangle. Carefully lift on to a baking sheet lined with nonstick baking paper and trim the edges of the rectangle. Using a ruler, cut the dough into 8 exact 9 cm (3¾ in) squares. Using a 7.5 cm (3¼ inch) star cutter, remove a star shape from each square (cook the stars separately if desired). Repeat with the second batch of dough on a second baking sheet.

Bake the squares in a preheated oven, 180°C (350°F), Gas Mark 4, for 5 minutes. Remove from the oven and scatter the crushed sweets into the cut-out star areas. Return to the oven for an additional 8–10 minutes until the gingerbread is lightly coloured and the sweets have melted to fill the stars. (If they haven't completely spread into the corners, use a cocktail stick to spread the syrup while it is still soft.) Re-cut the edges of the gingerbread squares to neaten them, then leave them on the baking sheets to cool.

Put the royal icing in a piping bag fitted with a plain nozzle. Pipe a line of icing along an inside edge of 4 of the cookies and press together to make 4 sides of a box shape. Make 3 more box shapes in the same way. Use the remaining icing in the bag to pipe decorative lines around the edges of the boxes. Leave in a cool place to set for at least 2 hours.

Place a nightlight on a small mat or coaster, light it and lower a gingerbread box over the top.

edible gifts

mincemeat

Makes **3 kg (6.5 lb)**
Preparation time **20–30
minutes**, plus standing

500 g (1 lb) **currants**,
chopped
500 g (1 lb) **sultanas**,
chopped
500 g (1 lb) **seedless raisins**,
chopped
500 g (1 lb) **cut mixed peel**
125 g (4 oz) **blanched
almonds**, finely chopped
500 g (1 lb) **cooking apples**,
peeled, cored and coarsely
grated
500 g (1 lb) **soft dark brown
sugar**
250 g (8 oz) **shredded suet**,
chopped
1 teaspoon **ground nutmeg**
or grated **nutmeg**
1 teaspoon **ground cinnamon**
1 teaspoon **ground mixed
spice**
grated rind of 2 **lemons**
juice of 1 **lemon**
2–4 tablespoons **brandy**

Put the currants, sultanas, raisins, peel and almonds
into a large bowl. Add the apples, sugar, suet, spices
and lemon rind and juice and stir to mix thoroughly.

Cover the bowl with clingfilm and leave the mincemeat
to stand for 2 days.

Stir the mincemeat again very thoroughly, pouring off
any excess liquid. Stir in the brandy.

Pack the mincemeat into warm, dry, sterilized jars (see
page 9). Cover each jar with a disc of waxed paper,
waxed side down, then leave until cold. Top the jars
with cellophane covers or airtight lids. Label and store
in a cool, dry place for at least 2 weeks before using.
It will keep, unopened, for up to 6 months.

For cranberry mincemeat, use 400 g (13 oz) each
currants, sultanas and seedless raisins and make
up the quantity with 300 g (10 oz) dried cranberries.
Continue with the recipe as above.

ginger marmalade

Makes **2.25 kg (5 lb)**
Preparation time **30 minutes**,
  plus standing
Cooking time **2¾ hours**

8 **lemons**
2 large **oranges**
2.5 litres (4 pints) **water**
125 g (4 oz) **fresh root
  ginger**, sliced and finely
  shredded
1.5 kg (3 lb) **sugar**

Pare the rind thinly from the fruits and cut into fine shreds. Halve the fruits and squeeze out the juice, then put the juice and rind into a large pan with the measured water and ginger.

Chop the fruit halves, including the pith, and tie the pieces in a muslin bag. Add this to the pan and slowly bring the mixture to the boil. Reduce the heat, cover the pan and simmer for 2 hours or until the ginger and rind are completely tender. Take the pan off the heat and leave to stand until the muslin is cool enough to handle, then squeeze all the juices back into the marmalade and discard the bag.

Add the sugar to the pan and cook over a low heat, stirring continuously, until the sugar has dissolved. Increase the heat and bring to the boil, then boil hard to setting point. Using a slotted spoon, carefully skim off any scum, then leave the marmalade to stand for 15 minutes to allow the fruit to settle.

Stir well, then transfer to warm, dry, sterilized jars (see page 9). Cover each jar with a disc of waxed paper, waxed side down, then leave until cold. Top with cellophane covers or airtight lids. Label and store in a cool, dark place. It will keep, unopened, for 3–4 months.

For lime marmalade, wash and dry 6 limes and 2 lemons. Cut into quarters lengthways and then into long, very fine slices, removing all the pips. Mix the fruit in a large pan. Add 1.5 litres (2½ pints) water, bring to the boil, then reduce the heat, cover and simmer for 1½ hours. Add 1.5 kg (3 lb) sugar and proceed as above.

lime & passion fruit curd

Makes **1 kg (2 lb)**
Preparation time **15 minutes**
Cooking time **30–40 minutes**

250 g (8 oz) **caster sugar**
finely grated rind and juice of
  4 limes
125 g (4 oz) **unsalted butter**,
  cut into pieces
4 eggs, beaten
3 **passion fruits**

Pour a little water into a pan and bring to the boil. Stand a large heatproof bowl over the top, making sure that the base of the bowl is not touching the water. Put the sugar and lime rind in the bowl and press them against the edge of the bowl with a wooden spoon to release the oils from the rind.

Pour the lime juice into the bowl through a sieve and add the butter. Heat, stirring occasionally, until the butter has melted. Strain the eggs into the mixture and stir until well mixed. Continue heating gently for 20–30 minutes, stirring occasionally, until very thick. Take the bowl off the pan.

Halve the passion fruits, then scoop out the seeds into the lime curd using a teaspoon. Mix together gently.

Transfer to warm, dry, sterilized jars (see page 9). Cover each jar with a disc of waxed paper, placed waxed side down. Allow to cool, then cover the jars with cellophane covers or airtight lids. The curd will keep in the refrigerator for up to 1 month.

For lemon curd, omit the limes and use 2½ lemons instead. Continue with the recipe as above, omitting the passion fruits.

For mixed citrus curd, use 1 lemon, 1 orange and 1 lime instead of the 4 limes. Continue as above, omitting the passion fruits.

peach & date chutney

Makes **1.5–2 kg (3–4½ lb)**
Preparation time **10 minutes**
Cooking time **50 minutes**

12 **peaches**
500 g (1 lb) **onions**
2 **garlic cloves**, crushed
2 tablespoons grated **fresh root ginger**
125 g (4 oz) **pitted dates**, chopped
250 g (8 oz) **demerara sugar**
300 ml (½ pint) **red wine vinegar**
salt and **pepper**

Place the peaches in a large bowl, cover with boiling water and leave to stand for about 1 minute, then drain and peel them. Halve and pit the peaches and cut the flesh into thick slices.

Put the onions in a pan with the peach slices, garlic, ginger, dates, sugar and vinegar. Add a generous sprinkling of salt and pepper and bring the mixture to the boil, stirring continuously, until the sugar has completely dissolved.

Reduce the heat, cover the saucepan and simmer, stirring frequently, for 45 minutes, until the chutney has thickened.

Transfer the chutney to warm, dry, sterilized jars (see page 9). Cover the surface of each with a disc of waxed paper, waxed side down. When cool, seal with an airtight lid. Label the jars and leave to mature in a cool, dark place for 2 weeks before using. It will keep, unopened, for 6–12 months.

For apricot & date chutney, omit the 12 peaches and use 2 kg (4½ lb) apricots instead. Continue with the recipe as above.

tomato & pepper relish

Makes **2 kg (4½ lb)**
Preparation time **20 minutes**
Cooking time **35 minutes**

1 kg (2 lb) ripe **tomatoes**,
  skinned and chopped
1 kg (2 lb) **red peppers**,
  cored, deseeded and finely
  chopped
500 g (1 lb) **onions**, finely
  chopped
2 **red chillies**, deseeded and
  finely chopped
450 ml (¾ pint) **red wine
  vinegar**
175 g (6 oz) **soft light brown
  sugar**
4 tablespoons **mustard seeds**
2 tablespoons **celery seeds**
1 tablespoon **paprika**
2 teaspoons **salt**
2 teaspoons **pepper**

Combine all the ingredients in a large saucepan.
Bring the mixture to the boil over a moderate heat,
then reduce the heat and simmer, uncovered, for about
30 minutes until most of the liquid has evaporated and
the relish has a thick, pulpy consistency. Stir frequently
as the relish thickens.

Transfer the relish to 3 warm, dry, sterilized 500 g
(1 lb) jars (see page 9). Cover the surface of each
with a disc of waxed paper, waxed side down. When
cool, seal with an airtight lid. Label the jars and store
in a cool, dry place. The relish will keep, unopened, for
up to 3 months.

For beetroot & apple relish, put 500 g (1 lb) cooking
apples, peeled, cored and grated, and 500 g (1 lb)
grated raw beetroot in a large pan with 375 g (12 oz)
finely chopped onions, 1 tablespoon finely chopped
fresh root ginger, 2 crushed large garlic cloves,
1 teaspoon paprika, 1 teaspoon ground turmeric,
1 cinnamon stick, 250 g (8 oz) soft dark brown sugar
and 450 ml (¾ pint) red wine vinegar. Bring to the
boil, reduce the heat and cover. Simmer, stirring
occasionally, for about 1½ hours, until the relish has
thickened and the beetroot is tender. Jar, cool and seal
as above and leave to mature in a cool, dark place for
1 week. (It will keep, unopened, for 6–9 months.)

blueberries in kirsch

Makes **500 g (1 lb)**
Preparation time **10 minutes**,
  plus standing

375 g (12 oz) **blueberries**,
  destalked, very soft ones
  discarded
125 g (4 oz) **caster sugar**
200 ml (7 fl oz) **kirsch**

Prick each blueberry with a fork, then layer the blueberries in a clean, dry jar, sprinkling each layer with some of the sugar.

Pour the kirsch over the sugared blueberries. Seal tightly and shake once or twice.

Leave in a cool place and turn the jar upside down every day for 4 days until the sugar has completely dissolved. Label the jar and leave to mature in a cool, dark place for 3–4 weeks before using. The blueberries will keep, unopened, for 6–12 months.

For cherries in kirsch, omit the blueberries and use 375 g (12 oz) fresh red or black pitted cherries instead. Continue as above.

spiced sloe gin

Makes **750 ml (1¼ pints)**
Preparation time **15 minutes**,
  plus standing

250 g (8 oz) **sloes**, stalks
  removed and soft ones
  discarded
125 g (4 oz) **caster sugar**
3 whole **cloves**
pared rind of 1 **orange**
1 **cinnamon stick**, halved
about 750 ml (1¼ pints)
  inexpensive **gin**

Prick each sloe with a fork and drop them into a clean, dry 1 litre (1¾ pint) wide-necked, screw-topped bottle.

Using a plastic funnel or a cone of paper, pour the sugar into the bottle. Stick the cloves into the orange rind and add to the bottle along with the halved cinnamon stick.

Pour in the gin, seal with an airtight top and turn the bottle upside down 2–3 times.

Stand the bottle in a cool place and turn it once a day for 7 days until the sugar has completely dissolved.

Label the bottle and leave to mature in a cool, dark place for 6 months or longer if you can (the longer you leave it the mellower and more delicious it will be). The sloes should be discarded before the gin is served.

For damson gin, omit the sloes and spices and use 250 g (8 oz) damsons instead. Continue as above. (It tastes deliciously boozy spooned on to ice cream.)

For damson vodka, omit the sloes, spices and gin and use 250 g (8 oz) damsons and about 750 ml (1¼ pints) vodka instead. Continue as above.

fruit & nut discs

Makes **18**

Preparation time **10 minutes**, plus setting

Cooking time **5 minutes**

100 g (3½ oz) **plain dark chocolate**, broken up

100 g (3½ oz) **milk chocolate**, broken up

100 g (3½ oz) **white chocolate**, broken up

125 g (4 oz) **mixed dried tropical fruits** (such as pineapple, mango, papaya, melon)

25 g (1 oz) **blanched almonds**

25 g (1 oz) **unblanched hazelnuts**

Melt the 3 chocolates in 3 separate heatproof bowls, each over a pan of gently simmering water. Spoon on to 3 separate sheets of nonstick baking paper and spread to 16 x 12 cm (6½ x 5 inch) rectangles.

Use a 5 cm (2 inch) round metal biscuit cutter to make 6 impressions in each chocolate rectangle to mark the edges of each disc.

Cut the dried fruits into small, flattish pieces and arrange them within the marked discs along with the nuts. Chill or leave in a cool place until the chocolate is set but not brittle.

Use the cutter to cut out the discs and carefully lift them from the paper. They will keep, in an airtight container in a cool place, for up to 1 month.

For berry & chocolate hearts, melt 200 g (7 oz) plain dark chocolate as above. Using an ice-cube tray with heart-shaped moulds, spoon in enough melted chocolate to half fill 8 of the holes. Sprinkle over 50 g (2 oz) mixed dried cranberries and blueberries, then top up with the remaining chocolate. Chill in the refrigerator for at least 1 hour before upturning the ice-cube tray to pop out the chocolates.

creamy pistachio toffee

Makes **30**
Preparation time **15 minutes**,
  plus setting
Cooking time **20 minutes**

300 g (10 oz) **granulated
  sugar**
300 ml (½ pint) **double cream**
25 g (1 oz) **unsalted butter**
50 g (2 oz) **pistachio nuts**,
  roughly chopped

Put the sugar and cream in a heavy-based saucepan and heat gently, stirring occasionally, until the sugar has completely dissolved. Stir the butter into the sugar and cream mixture, insert a sugar thermometer if you have one, and increase the heat. Cook for about 15 minutes until the temperature reaches 120°C (250°F) or a little of the toffee forms a hard ball when dropped into a bowl of cold water. Stir occasionally at first, then more frequently as the mixture begins to colour, froth and thicken. When the butter begins to separate out of the toffee, it is almost ready. Cook for a few more minutes until it changes to a smooth, glossy toffee.

Remove from the heat, quickly stir in the pistachio nuts, then pour the toffee into a greased 18 cm (7 inch) shallow square cake tin. Allow to cool for 5 minutes, then mark into strips and leave to cool completely.

Loosen the edges of the toffee from the sides of the tin and turn it out. Break into pieces with a toffee hammer or by hitting a cook's knife with a rolling pin. The toffee will keep, in an airtight container in a cool place, for up to 1 week.

For brazil nut & raisin toffee, use 300 g (10 oz) golden granulated sugar and replace the pistachios with 50 g (2 oz) roughly chopped brazil nuts and 25 g (1 oz) raisins. Otherwise proceed as above.

mint & chocolate fudge

Makes **800 g (1 lb 12 oz)**
Preparation time **15 minutes**,
  plus setting
Cooking time **5 minutes**

40 g (1½ oz) **strong
  peppermints**
500 g (1 lb) **plain dark
  chocolate**, chopped
400 g (13 oz) can **sweetened
  condensed milk**
50 g (2 oz) **milk chocolate** or
  white chocolate, melted

Place the peppermints in a polythene bag and crush them with a rolling pin, breaking them into small pieces. Continue to roll and flatten the mints until they are ground to a powder. Line a shallow 18 cm (7 inch) baking tin with nonstick baking paper.

Put the plain dark chocolate and condensed milk in a heatproof bowl over a pan of gently simmering water. Leave until melted, stirring frequently. When melted, stir in the ground peppermints.

Beat the mixture until the ingredients are combined then turn it into the tin, spreading it into the corners. Level the surface and leave to cool. Chill in the refrigerator for at least 2 hours.

Lift the fudge out of the tin and peel off the paper. Melt the milk or white chocolate in a heatproof bowl over a pan of gently simmering water, then place in a paper piping bag. Snip off the tip and scribble lines of chocolate over the fudge. When the chocolate is set, cut the fudge into 2 cm (¾ inch) squares. It will keep for up to 2 weeks in the refrigerator.

For coffee & orange chocolate fudge, omit the peppermints and instead add the finely grated rind of 1 small orange and 1 teaspoon instant espresso powder to the melted chocolate and condensed milk mixture. Continue as above.

chocolate & pine nut praline

Makes **225 g (7½ oz)**
Preparation time **15 minutes**,
    plus setting
Cooking time **10 minutes**

50 g (2 oz) **pine nuts**
25 g (1 oz) **flaked almonds**
200 g (7 oz) **caster sugar**
5 tablespoons **water**
50 g (2 oz) **plain dark
    chocolate**, broken into
    pieces

Lightly toast the pine nuts and almonds. Break up the nuts in a food processor or use a pestle and mortar until the nuts are broken into slightly smaller pieces, but not too finely ground.

Put the sugar and measured water in a small heavy-based saucepan and heat very gently, stirring until the sugar dissolves. Bring to the boil and cook, without stirring, until the syrup has turned to golden caramel. This will take 6–8 minutes. Immediately dip the base of the pan in cold water to prevent further cooking (if you overcook it, the resulting praline will taste bitter) and stir in the nuts.

Work quickly as you turn the praline on to a large lightly greased baking sheet, spreading it out in a thin layer before it starts to set. Leave for about 1 hour, until the praline is brittle.

Melt the chocolate in a heatproof bowl over a pan of gently simmering water. Break the praline into pieces and place on a wire rack. Drizzle with the melted chocolate, then leave to set. The praline will keep, in an airtight container in a cool place, for up to 1 week.

For chocolate & macadamia nut praline, toast 50 g (2 oz) unsalted macadamia nuts and 25 g (1 oz) chopped hazelnuts and use instead of the pine nuts and flaked almonds. Instead of drizzling melted plain dark chocolate over the praline, coat the pieces in 50 g (2 oz) melted milk chocolate and leave to set.

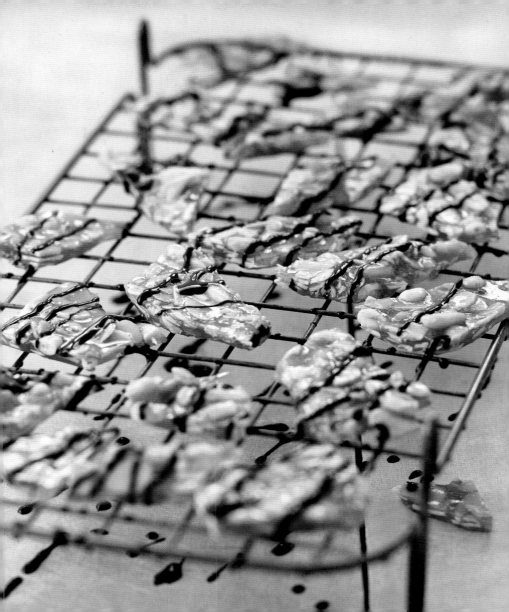

rocky road clusters

Makes **28**
Preparation time **40 minutes**,
  plus setting
Cooking time **10 minutes**

150 g (5 oz) **mixed whole
  nuts** (such as cashews,
  hazelnuts, pistachios)
300 g (10 oz) **plain dark
  chocolate**, broken into
  pieces
15 g (½ oz) **unsalted butter**
2 tablespoons **icing sugar**
2 tablespoons **double cream**

Put the nuts on a piece of foil on a baking sheet, then
toast under a preheated hot grill for 3–4 minutes until
golden. Allow to cool slightly, then chop roughly.

Melt 75 g (3 oz) of the chocolate in a heatproof bowl
over a pan of gently simmering water. Stir the butter,
sugar and cream into the melted chocolate until
smooth and glossy, then mix in all but 2 tablespoons
of the chopped nuts.

Drop teaspoons of the mixture on to a baking sheet
lined with nonstick baking paper. Chill for 2–3 hours
until the mixture is firm.

Melt the remaining chocolate as before. Coat the nut
clusters in the melted chocolate by holding them on
a fork, one at a time, over the bowl of chocolate and
spooning some of it over the top with a teaspoon.
When the excess chocolate has dripped away, return
the cluster to the paper-lined tray and repeat with
the remainder.

Put the chocolates in a cool place and leave to set
for at least 1 hour, then sprinkle with the reserved nuts.
They will keep in the refrigerator for up to 4 days.

For white chocolate clusters, reduce the quantity
of mixed whole nuts to 125 g (4 oz). Melt 75 g (3 oz)
white chocolate instead of the plain dark chocolate
and stir in the butter, sugar, cream and nuts as above.
Drop spoonfuls of the mixture on to a baking sheet,
chill and dust with 2 tablespoons sieved golden icing
sugar to finish.

white chocolate mint truffles

Makes **20**
Preparation time **30 minutes**,
  plus cooling and setting
Cooking time **4–5 minutes**

125 ml (4 fl oz) **double cream**
150 g (5 oz) **white chocolate**,
  broken into pieces
25 g (1 oz) **strong, hard,
  white peppermints**
40 g (1½ oz) **icing sugar**

Pour the cream into a heavy-based saucepan and add the chocolate. Heat gently, stirring occasionally, for about 4–5 minutes, until the chocolate has melted. Allow to cool.

Whisk the cream mixture until thick, then chill in the refrigerator for 3–4 hours.

Put the peppermints into a plastic bag, crush them with a rolling pin, then stir into the chilled cream mixture. Drop teaspoons of the soft mixture on to a plate and chill for 1 hour or freeze for 30 minutes until firm.

Sprinkle the icing sugar on to another plate, then roll the truffles in the sugar to form neat balls. When packed in the gift box, dust with the remaining sugar. Chill for at least 2 hours before using. The truffles will keep in the refrigerator for up to 4 days.

For chocolate rum truffles, melt 75 g (3 oz) plain dark chocolate in a heatproof bowl over a pan of simmering water. Remove from the heat. Beat 25 g (1 oz) unsalted butter and 125 g (4 oz) sifted icing sugar together until light and fluffy. Mix in the cooled, melted chocolate and 2 tablespoons dark rum. Chill until firm, then shape into 2.5 cm (1 inch) balls and roll each ball in cocoa powder. Makes about 16 truffles that will keep in the refrigerator for 2–3 weeks.

caramelized pecans

Makes **35**
Preparation time **40 minutes**
Cooking time **20 minutes**

50 g (2 oz) **blanched
  hazelnuts**
1 **dried egg white**
50 g (2 oz) **caster sugar**
125 g (4 oz) **pecan nuts**
225 g (7 oz) **granulated
  sugar**
65 ml (2½ fl oz) **water**

Place the hazelnuts on a baking sheet and grill under a preheated grill until lightly browned. Allow to cool slightly, then grind finely in a food processor or blender or crush using a pestle and mortar.

Reconstitute the egg white with warm water, according to the packet instructions, then add the caster sugar and ground hazelnuts and mix to a stiff marzipan paste. Sandwich the pecan nuts together in pairs with a little of the hazelnut marzipan.

Put the granulated sugar and measured water in a heavy-based saucepan and heat gently, without stirring, until the sugar has completely dissolved. Increase the heat and cook for 10–15 minutes until the syrup has turned golden.

Plunge the base of the pan into a bowl of cold water to prevent the syrup from cooking and darkening further. Drop the sandwiched pecan nuts, one at a time, into the caramel. Lift out with a fork and leave on a greased baking sheet to cool and harden. They will keep, in an airtight container in a cool place, for up to 4 days.

For marzipan walnuts, use 125 g (4 oz) walnut halves instead of the pecans. Omit the caramel glazing and instead sandwich the walnut halves together with a little of the hazelnut marzipan.

cranberry blondies

Makes **20**
Preparation time **25 minutes**
Cooking time **30–35 minutes**

200 g (7 oz) **white chocolate**, broken into pieces
125 g (4 oz) **unsalted butter**
3 **eggs**
175 g (6 oz) **caster sugar**
1 teaspoon **vanilla extract**
150 g (5 oz) **plain flour**
1 teaspoon **baking powder**
75 g (3 oz) **dried cranberries**

Line an 18 x 28 x 5 cm (7 x 11 x 2 inch) roasting tin with nonstick baking paper and snip diagonally into the corners so that the paper fits snugly.

Melt half the chocolate and the butter in a heatproof bowl over a pan of gently simmering water. Whisk the eggs, sugar and vanilla extract in a separate bowl with an electric whisk until light and frothy and the whisk leaves a trail when lifted.

Fold the chocolate and butter mixture into the beaten eggs with a metal spoon. Sift the flour and baking powder over the top and then fold in gently. Chop the remaining chocolate and fold half of it into the mixture with half the cranberries.

Pour the mixture into the tin and sprinkle with the remaining chocolate and cranberries. Bake in a preheated oven, 180°C (350°F), Gas Mark 4, for 30–35 minutes until well risen. Leave to cool in the tin.

Lift out of the tin, peel off the paper and cut the cake into squares. The blondies will keep, in an airtight container in a cool place, for a few days.

For rum & raisin chocolate brownies, use 200 g (7 oz) plain dark chocolate in place of the white chocolate and omit the vanilla extract. Replace the cranberries with 75 g (3 oz) raisins, soaked overnight in 3 tablespoons rum. If liked, drizzle the cake with melted milk chocolate before cutting into squares.

quick hazelnut melts

Makes **20**
Preparation time **10 minutes**
Cooking time **15 minutes**

50 g (2 oz) **blanched hazelnuts**
125 g (4 oz) **unsalted butter**, softened
50 g (2 oz) **caster sugar**
150 g (5 oz) **plain flour**

Grind the hazelnuts in a food processor or blender, or crush using a pestle and mortar, until fairly smooth but still retaining a little texture. Brown in a heavy-based frying pan over a low heat until evenly golden. Pour into a bowl and stir until cool.

Beat the butter and sugar together until the mixture is creamy. Add the flour and cooled nuts and mix well to form a soft dough.

Shape walnut-sized pieces of dough into balls, then pat into flat ovals. Place on a greased baking sheet and flatten slightly with a fork.

Bake in a preheated oven, 190°C (375°F), Gas Mark 5, for 12 minutes, until just golden. Cool on a wire rack. They will keep, in an airtight container in a cool place, for a few days.

For almond hearts, beat 250 g (8 oz) softened butter with 125 g (4 oz) sifted icing sugar and 1 egg yolk until pale and creamy. Add 125 g (4 oz) ground almonds and 375 g (12 oz) sifted plain flour and knead to a firm dough. Shape into a ball, wrap in clingfilm and refrigerate for 2 hours. Roll out to 5 mm (¼ inch) thick and use a heart-shaped cutter to make 40 hearts. Place on a baking sheet, brush with beaten yolk and top each heart with a blanched almond half. Bake at 200° (400°F), Gas Mark 6, for 10–12 minutes. Cool on the baking sheet for 5 minutes, then transfer to a wire rack.

chocolate ring cookies

Makes **16**
Preparation time **40 minutes**,
 plus chilling and cooling
Cooking time **15 minutes**

250 g (8 oz) **plain flour**
25 g (1 oz) **cocoa powder**
250 g (8 oz) chilled **unsalted butter**, diced
140 g (4½ oz) **icing sugar**
2 **egg yolks**
2 teaspoons **vanilla extract**
125 g (4 oz) **white chocolate**,
 broken into pieces
75 g (3 oz) **plain dark chocolate**, in a block
75 g (3 oz) **unblanched hazelnuts**, roughly chopped
crystallized rose petals

Put the flour, cocoa powder and butter in a bowl and rub in with the fingertips until the mixture resembles fine breadcrumbs. Add the sugar, egg yolks and vanilla extract and mix to a smooth dough. Wrap and chill for at least 30 minutes before using.

Roll out the dough on a lightly floured surface, then cut out rounds using an 8.5 cm (3¾ inch) round biscuit cutter. Use a 3 cm (1¼ inch) round cutter to cut out the centres to make rings. Place on greased baking sheets, spaced slightly apart, and re-roll the trimmings to make extras. Bake in a preheated oven, 180°C (350°F), Gas Mark 4, for 15 minutes or until beginning to darken around the edges. Cool on a wire rack.

Melt the white chocolate in a heatproof bowl over a pan of gently simmering water. Using a potato peeler, pare off curls from the plain dark chocolate.

Drizzle a little white chocolate over each cookie and scatter with some hazelnuts, rose petals and dark chocolate curls. Leave in a cool place to set for about 1 hour before using. They will keep, in an airtight container in a cool place, for a few days.

For vanilla ring cookies, make the cookies as above but omit the cocoa powder and add an extra 25 g (1 oz) flour. To decorate, drizzle the biscuits with melted plain dark chocolate and scatter with hazelnuts, crystallized rose petals and white chocolate curls.

thumbprint cookies

Makes **14**
Preparation time **20 minutes**
Cooking time **20 minutes**

125 g (4 oz) **unsalted butter**,
  softened
50 g (2 oz) **light brown sugar**
1 **egg**, separated
½ teaspoon **ground mixed
  spice**
100 g (3½ oz) **plain flour**
75 g (3 oz) **slivered almonds**,
  crushed
5 tablespoons **strawberry** or
  raspberry jam
icing sugar, for dusting
  (optional)

Beat the butter and brown sugar until creamy. Add the egg yolk, ground mixed spice and flour and mix to form a soft dough. Lightly beat the egg white to break it up and tip it on to a plate. Scatter the almonds on a separate plate.

Shape the dough into small balls, 3 cm (1¼ inches) in diameter, and roll them first in the egg white and then in the almonds until well coated.

Place the balls on a greased baking sheet, spaced slightly apart, and flatten slightly. Bake in a preheated oven, 180°C (350°F), Gas Mark 4, for 10 minutes, then remove from the oven. Allow to cool a little, then lightly flour your thumb and make a thumbprint in the centre of each cookie. Spoon a little jam into each cavity and return the cookies to the oven for an extra 10 minutes or until pale golden. Transfer to a wire rack to cool.

Dust the edges of the cookies with icing sugar, if liked. They will keep, in an airtight container in a cool place, for a few days.

For peanut butter thumbprint cookies, make the cookies as above, using 75 g (3 oz) crushed unsalted peanuts instead of the almonds. Fill the thumbprint cavities with smooth peanut butter instead of the jam.

traditional shortbread

Makes **8 pieces**
Preparation time **15 minutes**,
   plus chilling
Cooking time **45–60 minutes**

250 g (8 oz) **plain flour**
125 g (4 oz) **rice flour** or
   ground rice
125 g (4 oz) **caster sugar**,
   plus extra for dusting
pinch of **salt**
250 g (8 oz) **unsalted butter**,
   softened

Sift the 2 flours (or flour and rice), sugar and salt into a mixing bowl. Rub in the butter with your fingertips. When the mixture starts to bind, gather it with one hand into a ball. Knead it on a lightly floured surface to a soft, smooth, pliable dough.

Put the dough in a 20 cm (8 inch) flan ring set on a greased baking sheet. Press it out with your knuckles to fit the ring. Mark the shortbread into 8 pieces using the back of a knife. Prick right through to the baking sheet with a fork in a neat pattern. Cover and chill for at least 1 hour before baking, to firm it up.

Bake in a preheated oven, 150°C (300°F), Gas Mark 2, for 45–60 minutes, or until the shortbread is a pale biscuit colour but still soft. Remove the shortbread from the oven and leave to cool and shrink before removing the ring, then dust lightly with caster sugar. When cold, cut into 8 pieces. It will keep, in an airtight container in a cool place, for a few days.

For cinnamon shortbread, sift 150 g (5 oz) plain flour, a pinch of salt, 1 teaspoon ground cinnamon and 25 g (1 oz) ground rice into a bowl and stir in 50 g (2 oz) caster sugar. Rub in 125 g (4 oz) unsalted butter, then knead, shape, prick with a fork and chill as above. Bake in a preheated oven, 160°C (325°F), Gas Mark 3, for about 40 minutes or until pale golden. Leave on the baking sheet for 10 minutes, then cool on a wire rack.

linzertorte cookies

Makes **12**
Preparation time **30 minutes**,
  plus cooling
Cooking time **17 minutes**

125 g (4 oz) **unsalted butter**
125 g (4 oz) **caster sugar**
1 tablespoon **golden syrup**
75 g (3 oz) **rolled oats**
125 g (4 oz) **self-raising flour**
½ teaspoon **bicarbonate of
  soda**
4 tablespoons **raspberry jam**
275 g (9 oz) **white marzipan**
icing sugar, for dusting

Heat the butter, sugar and syrup gently until the butter has melted. Remove from the heat and mix in the oats, flour and bicarbonate of soda. Tip into a bowl and leave until cool enough to handle.

Shape the mixture into 12 balls. Space them well apart on a greased baking sheet and flatten each slightly. Bake in a preheated oven, 180°C (350°F), Gas Mark 4, for 15 minutes.

Spread a teaspoonful of jam over the centre of each cookie. Thinly roll out the marzipan on a surface lightly dusted with icing sugar and cut out 12 rounds, using a 8 cm (3½ inch) round biscuit cutter. Use a 5 cm (2 inch) round cutter to cut out the centre of each round. Re-roll the trimmings and cut into 5 mm x 5 cm (¼ x 2 inch) strips. Arrange 4 strips over each cookie to make a diamond pattern and place a ring of marzipan over the top. Cook under a preheated grill for about 2 minutes until golden, watching closely as the marzipan will brown very quickly.

Transfer to a wire rack to cool and dust the edges of the cookies with icing sugar. They will keep, in an airtight container in a cool place, for a few days.

For festive cookies, make the dough and shape into 12 balls as above. Flatten each to about 7.5 cm (3¼ inches) in diameter and space on a greased baking sheet. Arrange 50 g (2 oz) dried small soft fruits around the edge of each cookie, then top with 4 chopped glacé cherries, 1 tablespoon pumpkin seeds and 2 tablespoons slivered almonds. Bake as above, omitting the jam and marzipan stage.

leftover
turkey
ideas

turkey & chestnut soup

Serves **6**
Preparation time **20 minutes**
Cooking time **3½ hours**

1 **turkey carcass**
leftover stuffing (optional)
2 **onions**, finely chopped
2 **carrots**, finely chopped
2 **celery sticks**, finely
  chopped
1.8 litres (3 pints) **water**
cooked turkey, cut into bite-
  sized pieces
2 tablespoons **oil**
2 large **potatoes**, diced
475 g (15 oz) can **whole**
  chestnuts in brine, drained
3 tablespoons **sherry** or **port**
salt and **pepper**

Break the turkey carcass into pieces and place in a large saucepan with the stuffing, if using, and 1 onion, 1 carrot, 1 celery stick and the seasoning. Add the measured water and bring to the boil. Cover and simmer for 3 hours. Add extra water as necessary.

Remove the carcass and vegetables and discard. Strain the stock and add the turkey meat.

Heat the oil in the rinsed-out pan, then add the potatoes and the remaining onion, carrot and celery. Cook gently, stirring, for 5 minutes.

Pour in the turkey stock and bring to the boil. Simmer for 20 minutes, then add the chestnuts and sherry or port. Reheat and check the seasoning before serving.

For turkey & sweetcorn soup, omit the chestnuts and instead add a drained 325 g (11 oz) can of sweetcorn at the end of the cooking time. Warm through, season to taste and serve the soup garnished with 1 tablespoon chopped parsley.

rigatoni with turkey & pesto

Serves **3–4**
Preparation time **5 minutes**
Cooking time **10–15 minutes**

250 g (8 oz) **rigatoni**
½ teaspoon **salt**
2 tablespoons **extra virgin olive oil**
375 g (12 oz) **cooked turkey**, cut diagonally into thin strips
3 tablespoons **green pesto**
4–6 tablespoons **double cream**
salt and **pepper**

To garnish
freshly grated **Parmesan cheese**
basil leaves

Cook the pasta in a large saucepan of boiling water with the salt and 1 tablespoon of the oil for about 10 minutes, or according to the packet instructions, until al dente.

Heat a wok or large deep frying pan over a moderate heat until hot, then add 1 tablespoon oil and heat until hot but not smoking. Add the turkey and stir-fry for 1–2 minutes.

Add the pesto and continue to stir-fry for 2–3 minutes until the turkey is heated through.

Drain the pasta well, add to the turkey mixture and toss over a high heat until evenly mixed with the turkey and pesto. Add the cream, season to taste and stir well to mix. Serve garnished with Parmesan and basil.

For penne with turkey & red pesto, replace the rigatoni with 250 g (8 oz) penne and replace the green pesto with 3 tablespoons red pesto. Add 75 g (3 oz) pitted black olives to the turkey and pasta mixture and heat through before serving.

turkey & green pepper stir-fry

Serves **4**
Preparation time **15 minutes**
Cooking time **10–15 minutes**

3 tablespoons **rapeseed oil**
50 g (2 oz) **pine nuts**
1 **onion**, thinly sliced
2.5 cm (1 inch) piece of **fresh root ginger**, very thinly sliced
2 **green peppers**, cored, deseeded and cut lengthways into thin strips
500 g (1 lb) **cooked turkey**, cut diagonally into thin strips
salt and **pepper**

Sauce
2 teaspoons **cornflour**
2 tablespoons **water**
2 tablespoons **soy sauce**
2 tablespoons **rice wine** or **dry sherry**
1 tablespoon **wine vinegar**
1 **garlic clove**, crushed
1 teaspoon **soft dark brown sugar**

Blend the cornflour and measured water, add the remaining sauce ingredients and set aside.

Heat 1 tablespoon of the oil in a wok, add the pine nuts and toss for 1–2 minutes until golden brown. Remove and drain on kitchen paper.

Stir-fry the onion, ginger and green peppers gently in the remaining oil for 3–4 minutes until softened but not coloured. Remove and set aside.

Stir-fry the turkey for 1–2 minutes until heated through.

Whisk the sauce, add to the wok and bring to the boil, stirring until thickened. Add the pepper mixture and stir well to mix, then stir in the pine nuts. Season to taste and serve with rice or noodles.

For turkey & mangetout stir-fry, heat 2 tablespoons oil and stir-fry a grated 2.5 cm (1 inch) piece of fresh root ginger and 2 sliced garlic cloves for 2 minutes. Add 1 roughly chopped onion and 125 g (4 oz) mangetout and stir-fry for 3 minutes. Add 500 g (1 lb) cooked turkey, cut into thin strips, 3–4 spring onions, cut into 2.5 cm (1 inch) lengths, and 3 tablespoons oyster sauce. Season lightly and stir-fry for 1–2 minutes until the turkey is heated through.

turkey tetrazzini

Serves **4**
Preparation time **10 minutes**
Cooking time **15 minutes**

250 g (8 oz) **spaghetti**
½ teaspoon **salt**
1 tablespoon **extra virgin olive oil**
40 g (1½ oz) **butter**
40 g (1½ oz) **plain flour**
600 ml (1 pint) **turkey** or **chicken stock**
125 ml (4 fl oz) **double cream**
good pinch of **mustard powder**
375 g (12 oz) **cooked turkey**, cut into thin strips
3 tablespoons freshly grated **Parmesan cheese**
salt and **pepper**

Cook the spaghetti in a large saucepan of boiling water with the salt and oil for 8–10 minutes, or according to the packet instructions, until al dente.

Melt the butter in a saucepan, sprinkle in the flour and cook over a moderate heat, stirring, for 1–2 minutes. Gradually pour in the stock, beating vigorously after each addition. Bring to the boil, stirring, then reduce the heat and simmer, stirring, for about 5 minutes until thick and smooth.

Remove from the heat, stir in the cream and mustard, and season to taste. Gently fold in the turkey strips.

Drain the spaghetti and spread half in the bottom of a lightly greased ovenproof dish. Cover with half the turkey mixture, then the remaining spaghetti. Top with the remaining turkey and sprinkle with the Parmesan.

Place in a preheated oven, 200°C (400°F), Gas Mark 6, for 10 minutes or until golden.

For turkey pasticciata, use 175 g (6 oz) penne. Make a white sauce as above with 25 g (1 oz) each butter and flour and 600 ml (1 pint) milk. Remove from the heat, add 125 g (4 oz) diced mozzarella, 20 g (¾ oz) grated Parmesan, a pinch of nutmeg, salt and pepper. Mix the pasta with 250 g (8 oz) cooked turkey strips and add two-thirds of the cheese sauce. Pour into a baking dish. Mix 2 beaten eggs into the remaining sauce and pour over the top. Sprinkle with 20 g (¾ oz) grated Parmesan and bake in a preheated oven, 190°C (375°F), Gas Mark 5, for 20 minutes.

turkey & lentil salad

Serves **4**
Preparation time **10 minutes**, plus cooling
Cooking time **45 minutes**

250 g (8 oz) **puy lentils**
2 tablespoons **extra virgin olive oil**, plus extra to drizzle
1 **onion**, finely chopped
2 **red peppers**, cored, deseeded and finely sliced
2 **garlic cloves**, crushed
1 teaspoon **cumin seeds**
250 g (8 oz) **chestnut mushrooms**, sliced
rind and juice of 1 **lemon**
handful of **flat leaf parsley**
250 g (8 oz) **cooked turkey**, sliced
salt and **pepper**

Cook the lentils in a large saucepan of salted boiling water for 35–40 minutes, or according to the packet instructions, until cooked al dente. Drain and transfer to a large salad bowl.

Heat the olive oil in a frying pan and add the onion and red pepper. Cook over a medium heat for 15 minutes until beginning to soften, then add the garlic and cumin seeds and cook for 1 minute. Add the mushrooms, season with salt and pepper and cook for 2–3 minutes until they are softened.

Add the cooked vegetables to the warm lentils, stir in the lemon rind and juice and the parsley, and drizzle well with the oil. Season to taste. Allow the salad to cool to room temperature, then add the leftover turkey. Leave to marinate for at least 30 minutes before eating.

For turkey & penne salad, omit the lentils and instead cook 300 g (10 oz) penne in salted boiling water until al dente. Drain, refresh under cold running water and drain again. Prepare the vegetables as above, then stir into the pasta with 250 g (8 oz) cooked turkey, the lemon rind and juice and the parsley. Instead of drizzling with olive oil, stir in 5 tablespoons crème fraîche before serving.

turkey & almonds au gratin

Serves **4**
Preparation time **15 minutes**
Cooking time **40–50 minutes**

500 g (1 lb) **cooked turkey**,
  cut into bite-sized pieces
25 g (1 oz) **butter**
125 g (4 oz) **blanched
  almonds**
50 g (2 oz) **Parmesan
  cheese**, grated
4 tablespoons chopped
  parsley
75 g (3 oz) **brown
  breadcrumbs**

Cheese & spinach sauce
25 g (1 oz) **unsalted butter**
25 g (1 oz) **plain flour**
600 ml (1 pint) **milk**
50 g (2 oz) **Cheddar cheese**,
  grated
1 **garlic clove**, crushed
75 g (3 oz) **baby spinach**
salt and **pepper**

Arrange the turkey in a shallow ovenproof dish. Melt the butter in a saucepan, add the almonds and toss until they are golden. Sprinkle the nuts and butter over the turkey.

Melt the butter for the sauce in a saucepan. Sprinkle in the flour and cook, stirring, for 1–2 minutes. Add the milk, a little at a time, stirring after each addition, then simmer for 2 minutes. Add the Cheddar and garlic, season to taste and stir until the cheese has melted, then stir in the baby spinach.

Pour the sauce over the turkey, then mix together the Parmesan, parsley and breadcrumbs and sprinkle the mixture evenly over the turkey. Bake in a preheated oven, 160°C (325°F), Gas Mark 3, for 30–40 minutes until golden and bubbling.

For turkey, blue cheese & pine nuts au gratin,

substitute 150 g (5 oz) pine nuts for the blanched almonds. Omit the butter and toast the pine nuts under a preheated hot grill for a few minutes, shaking to prevent burning. Set aside 25 g (1 oz) toasted nuts and mix the rest with the turkey in an ovenproof dish. Make a cheese sauce as above, replacing the Cheddar with 50 g (2 oz) crumbled mild blue cheese. Assemble the dish and bake as above, sprinkling with the reserved toasted pine nuts to serve.

turkey curry

Serves **4**
Preparation time **10 minutes**
Cooking time **25 minutes**

4 tablespoons **vegetable oil**
1 **onion**, sliced
2.5 cm (1 inch) piece of **fresh root ginger**, finely chopped
2 **garlic cloves**, crushed
1 **red chilli**, cut into rounds
1 teaspoon **ground coriander**
1 teaspoon **ground cumin**
¼ teaspoon **ground turmeric**
100 ml (3½ fl oz) **water**
6 **tomatoes**, chopped
500 g (1 lb) **cooked turkey**, cubed
2 tablespoons **plain yogurt**
juice of 1 **lime**, plus extra wedges to serve
handful of **coriander leaves**
salt and **pepper**

Heat the oil in a large saucepan or wok and fry the onion for 8–10 minutes over a low heat, until it is soft and golden.

Add the ginger, garlic, chilli and spices to the pan and stir-fry for 1 minute. Pour in the measured water and the tomatoes, bring to the boil, reduce the heat a little and simmer for 5 minutes. Season with salt and pepper to taste, then stir in the turkey cubes.

Cover and simmer gently for 10 minutes, until piping hot. Remove from the heat, then stir in the yogurt, lime juice and coriander leaves. Serve with extra lime wedges and naan bread, if liked.

For turkey & spinach curry, follow the recipe above but omit the coriander leaves and instead stir 75 g (3 oz) baby spinach into the tomato sauce when adding the turkey. Complete the recipe as above, with yogurt and lime juice.

turkey waldorf

Serves **4**
Preparation time **20 minutes**

125 ml (4 fl oz) **mayonnaise**
2 tablespoons **lemon juice**,
  plus extra to taste
375 g (12 oz) **cooked turkey**,
  shredded
3 **celery sticks**, sliced thinly
75 g (3 oz) **shelled walnuts**,
  roughly chopped
50 g (2 oz) **raisins**
1 small **cos lettuce**, thickly
  shredded
2 **Red Delicious apples**
salt and **pepper**

Put the mayonnaise in a large bowl, add the lemon juice and stir well to mix. Add the turkey, celery, walnuts, raisins and lettuce leaves to the mayonnaise and mix well again.

Core and thinly slice the apples, then add immediately to the salad and stir well to coat. Season to taste and add more lemon juice, if liked.

For turkey curry mayonnaise, combine 500 g (1 lb) cooked diced turkey, 1 red dessert apple, cut into small dice, 25 g (1 oz) sultanas or raisins, 25 g (1 oz) roasted salted peanuts, 6 tablespoons mayonnaise, 1 teaspoon curry powder, ½ teaspoon mild chilli powder and 1 tablespoon lime or lemon juice. Mix thoroughly and season to taste. Serve the mayonnaise on a bed of crisp lettuce leaves, garnished with coriander leaves.

country turkey pie

Serves **6**
Preparation time **20 minutes**
Cooking time **35 minutes**

50 g (2 oz) **butter**
40 g (1½ oz) **plain flour**
750 ml (1¼ pints) **milk**
1½ **chicken stock cubes**,
  crumbled
½ teaspoon **Worcestershire
  sauce**
1½ tablespoons **dry sherry**
3 drops **Tabasco sauce**
375 g (12 oz) **cooked turkey**,
  diced
175 g (6 oz) **mushrooms**,
  sliced
250 g (8 oz) **carrots**, cooked
  and sliced
250 g (8 oz) **button onions**,
  boiled
2 tablespoons chopped
  parsley
300 g (10 oz) **ready-made
  puff pastry**, defrosted if
  frozen
a little **flour**, for dusting
beaten **egg**, to glaze
salt

Melt the butter in a large saucepan, sprinkle in the flour and cook for 1 minute. Add the milk, a little at a time, stirring after each addition, then add the stock cubes and Worcestershire sauce and season with salt. Bring to the boil, stirring with a wooden spoon until the mixture thickens. Stir in the sherry and Tabasco sauce. Add the turkey, mushrooms, carrots and onions and heat through gently but thoroughly. Stir through the chopped parsley, then turn the mixture into a 1.8 litre (3 pint) pie dish.

Roll out the pastry on a lightly floured surface and cover the dish, fluting the pastry edges. Make a small hole in the centre to let the steam escape. Decorate with the trimmings. Bake in a preheated oven, 200°C (400°F), Gas Mark 6, for about 20 minutes until the pastry is beginning to brown.

Brush the pie top with beaten egg, then return to the oven for a further 10 minutes until the pastry is puffed up and brown.

For turkey, ham & almond pie, brown 25 g (1 oz) almonds in 40 g (1½ oz) butter. Stir in 25 g (1 oz) plain flour, remove from the heat and stir until blended. Add 150 ml (¼ pint) dry white wine and 300 ml (½ pint) chicken stock, bring to the boil, reduce the heat and simmer for 1–2 minutes. Season well, then stir in ½ teaspoon dried marjoram and 2 tablespoons soured cream. Turn into 1.8 litre (3 pint) pie dish. Mix in 375 g (12 oz) diced cooked turkey, 125 g (4 oz) diced ham and 125 g (4 oz) halved seedless grapes. Cover and bake as above.

turkey sandwich

Serves **4**
Preparation time **10 minutes**
Cooking time **5 minutes**

8 **streaky bacon rashers**
8 slices of **wholemeal bread**
good-quality mayonnaise, for
  spreading
2 ripe **tomatoes**, sliced
small bunch of **watercress**
1 small ripe **avocado**, sliced
8 slices of **cooked turkey
  breast**
salt and **pepper**

Grill the bacon for 3–4 minutes on each side until golden and crisp. At the same time, toast the bread.

Spread 4 toast slices thickly with mayonnaise. Layer the tomatoes and watercress on top and add the avocado and turkey. Season well with salt and pepper and top with the crispy bacon. Cover with the remaining toast and press down lightly. Serve at once.

For turkey wraps, replace the bread with 8 tortillas and the watercress with 2 little gem lettuces. Chop the crispy bacon, finely chop the tomatoes and shred the lettuces. Mix together with 2 tablespoons soured cream, a splash of Tabasco sauce and a pinch of salt. Mash the avocado with the juice of 1 lime. Warm the tortillas under the grill or in the oven, then spread with the mashed avocado, a spoonful of the bacon mixture and a slice of turkey. Roll tightly and serve at once.

index

acknowledgements

The publisher would like to thank Copas Traditional Turkeys (www.copasturkeys.co.uk) and Goodman's Geese (www.goodmansgeese.co.uk) for supplying the traditionally reared free-range turkeys and geese shown in the photographs.

Executive editor: Nicky Hill
Senior editor: Fiona Robertson
Executive art editor: Sally Bond
Designer: Janis Utton
Photographer: Lis Parsons
Food stylists: Marina Filippelli and Joanna Farrow
Prop stylist: Liz Hippisley
Production controller: Carolin Stransky

Special photography: © Octopus Publishing Group Limited/Lis Parsons

Other photography: © Octopus Publishing Group Limited/Ian Wallace 89; /Jean Cazals 93, 119, 123, 125, 145, 153, 157, 163, 211; /Lis Parsons 131, 169, 171, 179, 191, 197, 199, 201, 203, 205, 207, 209, 213; /Stephen Conroy 193